Food Booth

The Entrepreneur's Complete Guide
to the Food Concession Business

Food Booth

The Entrepreneur's Complete Guide to the Food Concession Business

BARB FITZGERALD

Carnival Press
CORNELIUS, OREGON

First printing 2007
ISBN: 978-0-9765703-2-5
LCCN: 2007921853

ATTENTION CORPORATIONS, UNIVERSITIES, COLLEGES, AND PROFES-SIONAL ORGANIZATIONS: Quantity discounts are available on bulk purchases of this book for educational, gift purposes, or as premiums for increasing magazine subscriptions or renewals. Special books or book excerpts can also be created to fit specific needs. For information, please contact Carnival Press, P.O. Box 1068, Cornelius, OR 97113; ph 800-376-5074; carnival@foodbooth.net.

DEDICATION

This book is dedicated to my wonderful daughter Megan, whose presence and un-failing support have made this business the huge success and absolute joy that it has been for me. Thanks, Sweetie.

Sweetie—hard at work in 1989

DISCLAIMER

Every effort has been made to make this manual as accurate as possible based on the author's prior experience in the food concession business. The information provided is limited to the author's subjective opinion and should be used as a general guide; it is not to be considered an absolute authority. The author does not claim to understand thoroughly, to have interpreted properly, or to possess complete knowledge of any of the legal implications that may exist with regard to government rules, regulations, and restrictions. For legal and other expert assistance, you should seek the services of a competent professional.

All final legal, financial, and business decisions of significant importance are the sole responsibility of the reader. The food concession business is not a get-rich-quick scheme. Anyone starting a concession business must expect to invest a lot of time, effort, and money.

Every effort has been made to provide as complete and accurate information as possible. However, there may be mistakes both in the content and the typography. Therefore, this text should be used only as a general guide.

The purpose of this manual is to provide general information and suggestions. The author and Carnival Press have neither liability nor responsibility to any person or entity with respect to any loss or damage caused, or alleged to have caused, directly or indirectly by the content of this book.

TABLE OF CONTENTS

_____

Comparing Permanent and Temporary Concessions
Permanent Concessions Defined
Temporary Concessions Defined

Do Your Homework
Define Your Goal
Developing a Good Business Plan
Calculating Profitability

Your Business Identity
The Health Department in Depth
Permanent Concession Licensing
Temporary Concession Licensing
Your Food Handler's Card
Other Permits
Insurance

PART 2: Planning Your Booth and Equipment

Don't Forget the Miscellaneous Supplies
Loading Up

Setting Up at Your First Event
Your Booth Location, Location, Location
Who Has Seniority?
Health Department Inspections
Hiring and Managing a Staff

Signs Sell
Product Quality
Promote Sales with Good Presentation
Provide Quality Customer Service
Setting Prices
Efficiency for Maximizing Sales
The Benefits of Repeated Events
Competing on the Midway
Unethical Marketing
Operations and Managing Your Business

Bank Accounts
Get Organized

What's in It for You?

Two years ago, I published my first book, *Food Booth: The Complete Guide to Starting and Operating a Food Concession Business*. Each year it was expanded and revised with more complete information gleaned from my own research, input from other concessionaires, and feedback I'd received from readers. The book was well received and became a mainstay for those entering the concession profession. Because the book in your hands incorporates the features of the first book with a personal look at the day-to-day routine of a concession operation and contains the most up-to-date information possible, it merits at least a new subtitle. Since the publication of the first book, the concession business seems to have seen increased status for the profession. I'd like to credit my book for this progress; however, the change is more likely due to the public's evolving attitude and awareness of alternative forms of entrepreneurship. More people are rightfully viewing the concession business as a legitimate and respectable enterprise.

In the traditional sense, owning one's own business is the American dream. Unfortunately, for a variety of reasons, not everyone can do it. Inadequate capital, an inability to make a full-time commitment to the venture, or fear of financial risk are just some of the reasons many people don't reach for the golden ring of self-employment. People give up on the idea of being their own boss and instead commit their life to working for wages. However, some of these same individuals, such as students, retirees, and seasonal employees, have taken an unusual path to financial independence. They've found their niche as

1

concessionaires selling food at special events. The unique possibility of making a relatively large amount of money in a short period of time, a moderate investment of time and capital, and the ambiguity of a cash business with minimal licensing requirements are some of the unique benefits that make the concession business accessible and attractive to people who otherwise would not consider themselves to be entrepreneurs. The food concession business is also fun! What could be better than making money while spending time in the relaxed and fun atmosphere of special events?

But the inside world of the food concession business is a very well-guarded secret. There are no trade associations or library books to help guide the newcomer carefully past the start-up obstacles. Additionally, concessionaires are inherently reticent about providing information that could encourage newcomers to enter the field.

This book is written for the many people who have considered starting a food concession business. Perhaps these people were waiting in line for food at a fair when it occurred to them that they, too, could make money by selling food from a food booth. They attend events hoping to glean information from me and many other vendors, only to learn that most vendors are reluctant to divulge trade secrets. From those who are willing to share their expertise, they quickly realize there is more to this business than they had originally thought. They soon learn that comprehensive information about the concession business is virtually nonexistent. For them the choice is left either to start the business without adequate information or to do nothing. If you recognize yourself in this description, then this book is for you.

Nonprofit fundraisers will equally benefit from this book. Though a nonprofit is not venturing a business start-up, it is faced with the same challenges of maximizing sales and must compete in the same arena as professional concessionaires.

Let me begin by saying that I am a concessionaire. I have been a concessionaire for over twenty years. I have written this book about what I know about the concession business.

Please keep in mind that the information in this book is based on my personal experience of working events in Oregon and Washington. Permit and licensing requirements vary from state to state, as do regional food preferences and event protocol. This book represents my own personal perspective. Although I consider myself to be a typical vendor, others in the business may offer a very different point of view. Every concessionaire has a unique background and approaches the business differently. There is nothing consistent or certain about the food concession business. The whole affair is dictated by an ever-changing set of circumstances; therefore, this book is composed of generalizations. Over time you will develop your own theory of what does and does not make a successful concession business.

You have often heard that to be self-employed one must be willing to spend extraordinarily long hours and make tremendous personal sacrifices in order to be successful. Most entrepreneurs are a slave to long hours, contracts, licensing regulations, arbitrary legislation, and high start-up costs. As a result, many entrepreneurs soon find themselves responsible for a small business while feeling even less independent and free than they previously felt as an employee. Soon, they regretfully miss the set work schedule, paid holidays, personal leave time, retirement and health insurance benefits, steady paycheck, and limited responsibilities they had with the conventional job they so eagerly left behind.

However, unlike a typical small business owner, a concessionaire never feels married to the business. Concessionaires work on their own schedule, at their own pace, doing as many or as few events as they want. Time spent devoted to earning a living is condensed into a three- or four-month period, leaving much of the year to do other things they enjoy. And the concession business never gets boring. Each new event offers new faces, places, and opportunities.

Nonetheless, the concessionaire also suffers some of the same disadvantages of self-employment as do other entrepreneurs. Most notable are lack of employer-paid benefits, such as retirement, health insurance, and paid leave. Additionally, some of the benefits of running a concession business can also have a negative flip side. Working the business for only half of the year is only an advantage if you can pay your bills. Let's be honest. A concession business can only be considered successful if either entirely through it or with the assistance of other resources one is able to achieve financial security and stability.

Realistically, the only way to earn a good living with a concession is to work very hard at it. During the event season, concessionaires often feel they are running a marathon. For most of us, the summer is a long course of preparing for the event, stocking up, racing to the location, setting up, working the event, cleaning up, racing home or straight to the next event, stocking up, and so on. This hectic schedule is grueling. And it is also frequently a schedule that must be maintained while juggling the other responsibilities of family and home life.

The level of success from one vendor to the next varies tremendously. Many vendors never seem to get out of debt. These people live all winter on credit and spend the event season paying off their debts, only to start the cycle again the following winter. Many others don't earn enough to avoid the dreaded employment line. Some supplement their income during the winter with small indoor events or part-time jobs. However, there are some vendors who earn livings and even a few who manage to earn six-figure incomes entirely during the four-month event season. In January they might kindly send the rest of us a postcard from Baja.

There are three groups of food vendors. There are those who run small, easy-to-manage operations at small, easy events. Retirees, single operators, and people who use their concession part-time to supplement other income usually fall into this category. Another group consists of high-volume operators. They dedicate themselves to managing large amounts of equipment and quantities of inventory. They spend the season juggling employees and playing politics at large events. In the third category are the majority of vendors, who fall somewhere in-between. They earn enough to take several months off each year to do some home repairs or take a small vacation. Those with even a small source of supplemental income can generally survive the winter without depleting their savings accounts or spring start-up capital. And, in fact, many concessionaires use the winter months to enjoy the pursuit of other business ventures.

It requires several seasons to establish a schedule of good, high-producing events. Once established, a vendor's income level is mostly determined by one's menu, sales capacity, and ability and willingness to operate a high-volume operation.

Anyone can do this job. Well, almost anyone. It doesn't require a college degree or a background in food service or business management. You don't even need to be a good cook. However, a successful concessionaire must possess the ambition to take on the multitude of necessary tasks and see them through to the end of the season. It also requires that one be in reasonably good physical health. Starting a concession business requires an initial investment of capital for start-up costs, as well as a financial ability to manage through the first season of minimal returns while you learn the business and develop a schedule of productive events. It also requires an ability and willingness to wear many hats. Successful concessionaires act as their own finance managers, business managers, cooks, janitors, clerks, promoters, schedulers, bookkeepers, drivers, repairpersons, purchasers, and designers. The good news is: If you don't know how to do these things, you can learn. If you can't learn, you can find a partner or hire someone who possesses the skills you are lacking.

This is not a cookie-cutter job, and it's not a business for everyone. Everyone approaches the business with a different background, perspective, level of expertise, set of goals, and personal obstacles. The food concession business is not a get-rich-quick scheme, but rather a lifestyle. In that respect, it may take several years to find the life that is right for you. A new concessionaire needs to develop his or her concession businesses into one that is logistically comfortable, has a successful menu, and an established season of worthy events.

Starting a concession business is a life-altering experience. And yet today, as when I started, there are very few resources of vital comprehensive information to help new concessionaires conduct due diligence prior to making the investment or commitment. Without adequate information, the majority of new vendors start off blindly, become quickly discouraged, and quit after doing only a handful of events.

So let's get down to the bottom line, which is this: A typical, well-established concession business that serves a reasonably high-priced and high-volume menu through a season of good events can expect to earn what a typical, medium-wage worker would who is employed all year. No, you do not get rich. But the monetary difference between the two occupations is this:

- Your time investment is half of that at a regular job.

- This is a cash business.

- You get the tax benefits of being self-employed.

- You have the ability to be more financially flexible than you otherwise can be with the same amount of money, earned over a longer period of time.

There is no other profession I know of where you can get started so easily and inexpensively, make so much money, and have so much fun.

The information in this book is divided into four parts. The first section, Planning Your Business, addresses the process of due diligence. The second, Planning Your Booth and Equipment, is about the nuts and bolts of the business assets. The third, Events and Venues, addresses the particulars of finding and booking events. And the fourth, It's Showtime!, considers the activities of management, operations, and making money. Where appropriate, I have included photographs, accounting forms, sample applications, and work sheets for illustration and to keep you on track. These images and forms are to be considered examples, not endorsements. Finally, there's an appendix of resources at the back of the book to help you locate sources of outside information.

Whether your financial challenge is to create supplemental income or to develop your concession into a rewarding and prosperous career, I hope the information in this book will provide you with the insight you need to get started on the right foot toward many seasons of successful events. I mostly hope you enjoy the business and lifestyle as much as I do.

Part 1

Planning Your Business

CHAPTER 1

What Type of Concession
Is Right for You?

Comparing Permanent and Temporary Concessions

Unofficially, concession businesses fall into two categories, permanent and temporary. Actually, there is no official language to define the different types of concession businesses. Unlike folks in the medical profession who hang monikers like "Otorhinolaryngologist," to describe what they specifically do, we concessionaires describe our profession in full sentences. For example: "I'm a food concessionaire. During the summer I sell food from a food booth at fairs and festivals." So, for the purpose of explaining specific activities and licenses, I have taken the liberty of labeling these two types of concession businesses myself.

A *permanent concession* is essentially a conventional "storefront" operating full-time from a stationary location. Drive-thru espresso stands, coffee kiosks, storefront carts, and street corner vendors—to name just a few—are all considered permanent concessions. *Temporary or mobile concessions*, on the other hand, sell their product at a different location on a weekly basis. These concessionaires set up their booths at a variety of temporary events, such as fairs, festivals, sporting events, auctions, concerts, open-air markets, and special-interest events—nearly any place that a large group of people is gathered. A permanent concession, like any business, waits for customers to come to it whereas a temporary concession takes its business

9

to the customer from place to place. It's this transience that makes them very different.

The information in this book largely refers to temporary concessions. In order to create a better understanding of the unique nature of the food concession business, it's helpful to distinguish between the two further.

Permanent Concessions Defined

As with any storefront business, one factor that greatly determines the success of a permanent concession is its location. What makes a good location is determined by what you are selling and to whom you are selling. No matter your product and no matter your target market, your location must make your business visible and assessable to enough potential customers in order to profit. Good locations are extremely hard to find, and more often than not the good ones are already taken. If you do happen to find an opportunity to grab a good spot for your business, here are a few things to consider to help you decide if a permanent spot is right for you. I have organized these considerations into groups of positive and negative. Don't let my biases influence you. Although some people may hate certain aspects of a permanent concession, others may find these same aspects are just what they seek in their businesses.

Pros:

- *Stability.* The daily and weekly routine of opening, closing, and shopping for supplies.

- *A full-time schedule.* Working five, six, or seven days a week, year around, expands sales and creates a steady market base.

- *Familiarity.* Getting to know your steady customers can be very rewarding.

- *Operational ease.* Once the business is started, the daily operations are not difficult.

Cons:

- *Stability.* The daily and weekly routine of opening, closing, and shopping for supplies can make you feel like a slave to your business.

- *Time investment.* Running a business full-time requires a tremendous investment of time.

- *Commitment.* The hours of operation must remain consistent or sales will suffer. Your customers depend on you to be open during your regular hours. It can be difficult to take personal time away from your business.

- *Bureaucracy.* The visibility of a permanent concession requires a willingness to abide by all the governmental rules and red tape. Licensing requirements can be very involved.

- *Vulnerability.* Uncontrollable and unforeseen events can greatly impact and jeopardize your investment. Lease conflicts, road construction, and unforeseen competition are just a few of the many uncontrollable hazards that can ruin a business. If a location does not work well for you, it is extremely difficult to pick up and move your business to a new location.

- *Large initial investment.* It takes a relatively large amount of capital to start up any permanent concession business, no matter how small.

Temporary Concessions Defined

Location is an important factor for temporary concessions as well. The key difference is that whereas a permanent operation has the same location week after week, a temporary concession has a new location on a weekly basis, for good or bad. A permanent concession's sales will remain somewhat constant over time based on the quality of its location whereas a temporary concession's sales may vary widely as the quality of the event and location within each event change from week to week. For example, during one three-day event a temporary concession's sales might compare to those of a permanent concession that is open for business for an entire month. However, that same temporary concession may have minimal sales the following week from the following event. Additionally, while most permanent concessions are open for business year round, the temporary concession is only open for business for the length of the events during the event season. Here follows a list of additional considerations.

Pros:

- *The possibility* of making a relatively large amount of money in a short period of time.

- *Independence.* Complete control over nearly all aspects of your business decisions.

- *Limited time investment.* Most temporary concessions operate seasonally, enabling owners to spend time doing other things during the off-season.

- *Diluted risk.* If for any reason an event bombs, the next week provides a new event with new possibilities.

- *Variety.* Every event is different.

- *Autonomy.* The concession business is a cash business, has minimal licensing requirements, and is relatively unregulated.

- *Family.* Families who operate their concession together share the workload and spend time together. Young people gain confidence by learning a work ethic, responsibility, cash handling, and public relations skills. This could be the perfect family business.

- *Fun.* What could be better than earning a living in a relaxed and fun environment?

Cons:

- *Sale time limitations.* Annual earnings potential is condensed into a very short season of opportunity. What's worse, each event has a limited period of optimal selling time.

- *Risk.* Breakdowns, poor weather, poor health, low event turnout, faulty event organization, and employee no-shows are just some of the many things that can prevent an event from producing the way it should. This risk is magnified by the limited sale opportunities of the season.

- *Uncertain income.* High risk and event variability make it nearly impossible to calculate future income.

- *Lack of control.* Certain factors that greatly affect sales are uncontrollable. Most notable are weather, economy, and decisions made by the event coordinator, such as space location, duplication of menus, number of food booths, and poor planning.

- *Physical demands.* Stocking up, traveling to and from events, setting up, working the crowd, and tearing down are physically and mentally stressful. Doing these tasks repeatedly over the course of the season can be mentally and physically exhausting.

- *Stigma.* Generally, most people don't consider concessionaires to be legitimate small business owners but rather a cross between a "carny" (carnival worker) and a hobbyist.

Yes, the concession business is a gamble. As when considering the pursuit of any business venture, all of the factors should be weighed prior to making the investment.

CHAPTER 2

Getting Started Planning Your Business

Do Your Homework

To get a good start, proper research and planning are critical. Allow yourself at least a year prior to your first event to take all the necessary steps of researching, planning, equipping, and preparing to start your business off right. You will be more likely to succeed and less likely to have regrets if you have adequately prepared and can hit the ground running at your first event. Your goal in planning your new concession is to design a *booth* and *menu* that can be readily booked into *events* where you can make lots of *money*. Each of these four components is interrelated and will have an impact on each other throughout your concession career.

Visit some events. It is a good idea to attend some events before you start planning your business. By observing an event and the assorted booths at an event, you can get a lot of ideas for booth designs and menus. You can also get a feel for the various factors that determine the sales potential of the booths and of the event itself.

As you walk around, look at the event and booths from the viewpoints of both an attendee and a vendor. When you arrive, stand at the approach to the food court or midway. Take note which booths catch your eye, and ask yourself why. At each booth, note the booth's design and how visible, attractive, and clean it appears. How well can

15

you see inside? Note how many people are running it and if it is well organized. Pay attention to the menu. Is it well advertised with big, attractive, and easy-to-read signs or scribbled with a marker on poster board? Is the menu long and complicated or short and simple? If there are customers in line, note how quickly the line moves and, once they order, how long it takes them to receive their food. Be aware that a line of customers in front of a booth does not necessarily mean that the booth is making a lot of money. Also notice the price range of the menu. Is it "high ticket" or inexpensive? Are the customers mostly kids, adults, or both? It is a good idea to take photos and notes of booth designs, signs, and sign-hanging techniques for future reference.

Next, focus on the event from an attendee's point of view. Is it reasonably priced and well attended? Are the attractions bringing people in and keeping them there? Is it clean and well organized? Do you feel well rewarded for your time and money spent?

Now, look at the event from a vendor's point of view. Observe whether the booths are too close together or well spaced with ample room around each one. Pay attention to the flow of people. Note whether the booth layout provides equal sales opportunity for all booths, or are some booths much better positioned than others? Does the event appear to have more food booths than it needs or too few? Is there undue duplication of menus? Also, pay attention to the mood of the people attending. Do they generally appear to be shuffling around in a confused and frustrated fog, or are they upbeat, eager, and spending money? All of these factors and more will be addressed in detail in the following chapters.

Talk with event coordinators. Once you have designed your booth and menu, your ability to find a venue for your new business may depend on how well your business appeals to event coordinators. It would be wise to know upfront how to make your business as appealing as possible. Ask coordinators whether food booth space will be available for you at their next event. If not, find out why and what you can do to position yourself better for the next available space. Discuss which type of menu would be a welcome addition to their event.

Some coordinators are eager to shoehorn in a booth with an unusual menu. Coordinators can offer advice that will greatly improve your chances of finding good events.

Talk with concessionaires. Although your questions may not be well received, it doesn't hurt to ask. Most seasoned vendors are cautious about increasing the competition by encouraging new vendors. However, if approached correctly, they may be willing to offer advice. On many subjects, local vendors may be your only source of solid information. Any information you get about local bureaucracy and licensing requirements will be particularly valuable. Aside from specific questions you may have, it's always useful to ask vendors what things they regret in their planning or would change in their business. Here's a short list of reflections either I or other vendors have had:

- "Design my trailer with windows around the cooking area so I can see out."

- "Install the gray water tank in my trailer so that it drains on the right."

- "Purchase a larger truck for pulling my heavy trailer."

- "Been more careful in my hiring."

- "Purchased a smaller trailer."

- "Purchased a trailer with the service window on the driver's side, so it's easier to back into my space."

Educate yourself. Knowledge is power, as they say. You may be helped by taking classes at your local community college in subjects that will help you in your business, such as small business management, cooking, bookkeeping, auto maintenance, or welding. If you feel ignorant about certain aspects of running a business, go to the library or bookstore. Both are treasure troves of information. Contact the Internal Revenue Service (IRS) for publications about tax filing for a small business. Contact your state Economic and Community Development Department for small business resource guides. Or contact the Small Business Administration for a wealth of guidance, much available for free. Call them toll free at (800) 827-5722 or go online to www.sba.gov.

You may also want to join your state or regional fair association. Organizations like IAFA, International Association of Fairs and Expositions, NICA, National Independent Concessionaires Association, Inc., Western Fairs Association, or CAFÉ (Canada Association of Fairs and Expositions), as well as state associations are just some of the many organizations that provide networking, information, and insight into the concession industry. As a member, you also receive benefits, such as reduced insurance rates and discounts on everything from food products to paint. Even if you don't join, visit their websites for information about events, insurance, and links to other sites of interest. (See Appendix 3 for association references.)

Visiting a fair or festival is a good way to start researching your new venture.

Define Your Goal

When planning your concession business, you must first ask your-self several very important questions:

What is your purpose for starting a concession business? Are you a concerned baby boomer approaching retirement with an inadequate nest egg? Are you retired and wanting to stay active to earn an income? Are you looking for an excuse to do a little traveling? Perhaps you have some spare time in the summer and wish to use that time to supplement your winter income. Maybe you have teenage kids who need a fun way to earn college tuition. Are you semi-retired and need to supplement your fixed income? Maybe you have arrived at a large amount of money and see an opportunity to start your own business. Or maybe you are tired of scraping by as an employee and wish to become self-employed. Perhaps you are more or less unconcerned with making money, but simply looking for the tax advantages of being self-employed. Are you in charge of fund raising for an organization? Maybe you're simply a free spirit with a desire to be responsible for your own employment.

What do you ultimately expect to achieve from your concession business? How much is enough? Will an extra ten thousand dollars to invest provide you a more satisfying retirement? Will you be happy to earn enough to keep gas in the motor home while you satisfy your wanderlust? Perhaps an extra five or ten thousand dollars earned in your spare time will bridge the gap left by your inadequately paying "regular" job—or, better yet, will finally be enough to take that trip, remodel the house, or buy a new car. Maybe a summer concession business will keep the kids busy and help ensure that they receive a college education. Or perhaps you hope to quit your job eventually, make your living from your concession business, and use your spare time in the off-season to pursue other interests. Maybe you have been laid off and need to get your bills paid. Which brings me back to: How much is enough? Can you accomplish your goal if you finish the summer with five thousand dollars in your pocket? Or will it require seventy thousand dollars to feel fulfilled?

What are your financial resources? How financially capable are you of getting your concession started and seeing it through to the point where you have reached your goal? Do you have adequate resources available for start-up capital, as well as enough reserves available for the first season or two of low returns? If not, how do you propose to bridge the gap? Perhaps you will need to siphon small portions of your existing income into your new venture. Do you have enough income from a source other than your concession that will pay the bills until your concession becomes viable? Are your financial resources such that you can afford the appropriate booth, equipment, and vehicles to operate the concession you envision? Or perhaps you will need to equip your business conservatively and expand slowly as your business grows.

What are your capabilities for logistically seeing your plan through? Will you be juggling your time and energy with other responsibilities, such as parenting small children or working another job? Are you physically able to manage a long, grueling season of long hours on your feet and of lifting and carrying heavy objects? Do you have a partner, or are you willing to hire and manage adequate help? What type of skills do you have for driving large vehicles, pulling trailers, conducting vehicle and equipment maintenance, and managing a business?

These are the types of questions you need to ask before you get started. The answers to these questions will define the type of concession you will start with and the type of concession you will strive for. Your answers will also determine how long it will ultimately take you to reach your goal. If your goal is to supplement your already adequate income, then any profit made in the concession could be considered a success. On the other hand, if you yearn to replace the entirety of your current fifty-thousand-dollar-a-year salary, it could take a while longer and, depending on your resources, capabilities, and other responsibilities, may or may not be achievable. Although we would all like to make that kind of money from our concession, most vendors go through a process of learning while growing that eventually gets them to the point where they reach a personal balance between what is logistically comfortable and adequately prosperous. That said, if your goal was to earn a large income from your concession, you would likely have a difficult time reaching it if you aren't both capable and willing to strive for a high-volume operation.

A concession business with moderate expectations or financial and logistical limitations may be one that utilizes a small, inexpensive, and easy-to-manage booth to sell a small, easy-to-manage menu at small, inexpensive events. On the other hand, a concession operator whose goal is to make enough money to replace the entirety of an existing income may need to operate several high-volume booths through an entire season of large regional and state fairs. Many of these concessionaires spread their risk and optimize their returns by booking several different booths into different events on the same date.

A large number of concessionaires start out small with the goal of simply earning a little extra cash on the weekend. By the following spring, when they return for a new season, they have frequently quit their jobs and have much larger operations. They quickly learn that there is much more money to be made with their concession than they had originally thought possible.

A small, easy-to-manage booth.

Developing a Good Business Plan

Every successful entrepreneur starts with a plan. A thorough and complete business plan is not only a valuable tool for securing financing, but also a road map to help guide you through the essential elements of the business while helping you foresee and avoid potential problems. I don't recommend you start your business the way I did, without any planning or due diligence whatsoever. Although back then a person could get started relatively cheaply, I still lost many valuable years working out kinks by trial and error. Many of those errors were costly and could have been easily avoided with better critical thinking and a good business plan. The concession business as a whole is largely influenced by a wide array of variables, many of which are out of your control. A business plan makes you think through from start to finish every aspect of your business. Without careful analysis early on, unexpected costs or logistical complications can ruin your business. By developing a well-thought-out business plan, you can prepare yourself to roll with and survive the negatives, while positioning yourself to benefit from the positives.

Start with a plan outline to guide your research. As you progress, your plan will take shape. When it is complete, you will have absolute knowledge of what your business will involve before you make any investment. A comprehensive business plan for a mobile concession business should include the following:

Executive Summary

- General statement of purpose.
- Goals and objectives.
- Operation and product description.
- Operational logistics.
- Financial resources and summary.

Operations

Products. What are you going to sell? What are the logistical details of your menu? How will it be served?

Booth requirements and design. What type of booth will you use and how will it be acquired? What will your booth look like, be made of, and how will it be laid out?

Vehicle requirements. How many and what types of vehicles will you need for transporting your booth, equipment, inventory, and supplies. Will you need an extra vehicle for running errands? Will you or your helpers sleep in a vehicle?

Equipment requirements. What equipment will you need to prepare and serve your product?

Ingredients and product supplies. What are all the ingredients, condiments, and supplies you will need to serve your product?

Suppliers. Where will you buy your products and supplies? How convenient are they for you?

Inventory and supply transportation and storage requirements. How will you store your inventory and supplies before, during, and after an event? Storage capacity for all stock must be adequate for the size of your events and for ease of use. The storage and transportation requirement for your food products must be carefully analyzed to keep your food safe from contamination and spoilage.

Equipment transportation and storage requirements. How will you store your equipment before, during, and after an event? How will you transport your equipment to events?

License and insurance requirements. What types of licenses, permits, and insurance will you need? What are the regulations and requirements of each?

Small ware requirements. What small items do you need for preparing, serving, maintaining quality, and cleanup?

Market Strategy

Targeted customer profile. Will your menu appeal to children, adults, people with eclectic tastes, or folks who love standard fair food? Will your market be people who value quality over quantity or who are more concerned with quantity and price?

Event schedule profile. How many events, days, and months do you plan to work? How many days off do you need between events? Will you jump from one event to the next or go home between events? How far are you willing to travel?

Signs, and advertising. How do you plan to tell people what you are offering? How do you plan to compete with other booths at the event and other booths selling the same product?

Event contract procurement strategy. How do you plan to promote your services to event coordinators for the purposes of being offered a contract and to influence them favorably for any special needs you may have?

Product and service quality. What level of customer service will you provide? What degree of extra effort and cost are you willing to spend on quality?

Pricing. How much will you charge your customers for your product? What size portions will you serve?

Management and Staffing

Management qualifications. Who is in charge, and what are their qualifications?

Management functions. What are their jobs and responsibilities?

Staff requirements. How many helpers do you need, and when do you need them? How much will you pay them? Will they be considered employees or contract labor? What are their responsibilities? What sleeping arrangements will you provide them?

Staff procurement resources. Where will you find your staff? Do you have family or friends who will help, or will you need to hire from outside your circle of acquaintances?

Financial Analysis

Start-up costs. How much will it cost to put together and start your business? What is the cost of your booth, equipment, signs, and support vehicles?

Operating Costs. How much will it cost to operate your business from one event to the next? What is the cost of insurance, phone calls, interest payments, and maintenance? What is the cost of fueling your vehicles, paying for babysitters, space fees, licenses, and a staff of helpers?

Financial resources. How will you finance your business? Do you have adequate working capital? Do you have adequate capital reserves? If not, how do you propose to finance your start-up and operation?

Cost analysis. How much does you product cost? How much will each serving cost? What is the cost of each ingredient and paper product for each item on your menu?

One- to three-year profit/loss projections. What are your sales and expense projections for each event, for each season, and for three years?

Off-season financial resources. How will you support yourself during the off-season?

Risk Analysis

Potential areas of risk. In what areas are you most vulnerable? Poor health, poor vehicle or equipment condition, unavailability of helpers, etc.?

Risk reduction options. What possible solutions can you think of for your areas of risk?

Exit strategy. How will you recover your costs if you decide to get out of the business?

As you address each of the questions proposed in your business plan, the answer will likely lead to another question. Take the time to write everything down, and elaborate on your ideas.

Calculating Profitability

Ultimately, the most important question in your planning is: How much can you expect to earn? You can roughly get an idea by doing the math. For example, perhaps your goal is to earn a profit that would equate to a year's worth of wages. If you schedule ten events totaling thirty days of business, you would need to average $1,000 in sales a day to gross $30,000. If your total costs were fifty percent of your profits, you would then have profited by $15,000. Let's take the example further to determine if your menu and booth can accomplish this. Divide the price of an average serving into $1,000 (sales per day) to determine how many average servings you must sell each day to gross your $1,000. If $15,000 profit is a worthy target, then plan to ensure that every component of your business enables your concession to, at the very least, reach that goal.

10 Events = 30 days of business in season

Average sales per day	$1000
Days in season	x 30 days
= Revenue per season	$30,000
Revenue per season	$30,000
Cost of doing business	x 50%
= Net profit per season	$15,000
Average sales per day	$1000
Average price of sale	÷ $5
= Number of servings per day	200

On paper, two hundred sales per day for thirty days over the course of the season does not sound difficult, and it's not. Although some days those two hundred sales may be hard to secure, other days your sales may double or triple that amount. However, each unforeseen expense or setback during the season, perhaps in the form of a blown transmission or a rained-out event, will cause your goal to be further from reach. If your goal is to earn more than $15,000 during the season and you face considerable setbacks, you will probably need to make some changes to your plan. The easiest way to produce more revenue is to book more events.

Here's a tip: The concession business is unique in that, unlike other business start-ups, it is not an all-or-nothing proposition. A concession business can be customized to serve any size of goal, level of commitment, or level of financial return you wish.

However, if you find that your booth can't manage to average $1,000 a day in sales, you may need to consider other options. For some booths, $1,000 in sales a day is a cakewalk; for others, $1,000 for an entire event might be a stretch. Once you are familiar with the sales capacity of your booth, you should strategically select events that produce no less than your specific goal in sales. For example, a small single dish booth at a three-day event might be expected to earn no less than $2,000 in sales. For a large booth at the same event with a menu of four items and a staff of four, the minimum target might be $4,000 or even $8,000. If your sales can't reach your goal, you may need to make some very big changes to your business. You might consider changing your menu to a higher-priced dish, enlarging your menu, or enlarging your serving capacity.

CHAPTER 3

Licensing, Insurance, and Other Red Tape

Your Business Identity

To get a good start in the concession business, you may want to establish your business identity. Many vendors come up with a business name. The presentation of a name on event applications, health permit applications, and supplier credit applications goes a long way to establish a certain validity right upfront. It also goes a very long way toward helping you engage in a little positive visualization for yourself. Overcoming the stigma of not being considered a legitimate small business is, in some ways, as difficult for the vendor as it is for the public. As you try on a variety of names in the mirror, be aware that in many states if your business name is different from your last name, you will need to register the business name with the county clerk as your DBA (doing business as).

Another thing you might want to consider is whether to choose and to establish the legal organization of your business. The entity of your business has many tax filing and liability implications. Most vendors never give this subject a thought. And those who do may not do so until later in their concession career. If you choose to do nothing, the legal organization of your business automatically becomes a sole proprietorship.

A *sole proprietorship* is a business owned by one person or a married couple. In effect, you and your business are one. According to the

IRS, almost eighty percent of U.S. small businesses are sole proprietorships because it is the easiest and cheapest way to set up and run a business. There are no papers to sign, and you are free to run your business however you choose. The biggest disadvantage is that as a sole proprietor you have unlimited liability. If your business should be sued, all of your personal assets are at risk. Sole proprietors are also not able to have fringe benefits such as health insurance and disability insurance paid by the business. At tax time, business income is claimed on Schedule C and paid along with your personal income taxes.

A *partnership* consists of two or more people in business together. As with a sole proprietorship, the partners share unlimited liability. However, when it comes to taxes, they are treated separately from the business. A partnership needs to have a federal identification number issued by the IRS. Many states also require an identification number. At tax time the business files a tax return, but no taxes are paid with the return. Instead, each partner includes his or her share of the profits or losses on his or her individual tax return. The biggest disadvantage of a partnership is that each partner is bound by any business contracts that are signed by their business partners. Partnerships are notoriously risky and discouraged by many attorneys.

A *corporation* like a partnership is an entity separate from those who own it. Naturally, it is registered with the federal and state governments and must additionally pay an annual fee. Owners become shareholders and must adopt bylaws, elect officials, have meetings, and keep records. Taxes are involved and complicated. Owners are treated as employees and have taxes withheld from their paychecks. The benefits range from tax benefits, fringe benefit opportunities, and liability protection. I don't know any concessionaires who have their business incorporated, but I do know some who establish a limited liability company (LLC).

Limited Liability Companies can be established by a single-person or multi-person business by registering with the state. It is a fairly new entity that combines the advantages of a sole proprietorship with the advantages of a corporation. For federal tax purposes, the LLC is not treated as a separate entity from the owner(s), who will be either taxed as a sole proprietor or a partnership. Like those entities, the profits from the business are paid via the owner's individual tax returns. The advantage with an LLC—and what makes it popular with single-owner businesses—is that, like a corporation, the owners have limited personal liability for the business. In fact, liability is limited to the amount of the owner's investment in the business. However, (you knew there would be a catch!) some states have a special LLC tax, and in many states, an LLC is taxed as a corporation.

Of course, the subject of business entities is much more involved than stated here. Before rushing to a decision, sit down with an accountant and/or business attorney to get a thorough understanding of the ramifications of any decision you may make.

The Health Department in Depth

The health department, which is specific to the food service industry, issues the standard license of the concession business. Health department licensing regulations and requirements address two different but related aspects of a food concession business. One aspect that concerns the health department is the structural elements of the booth. For example, it may require a three-compartment sink, a plumbed hand washing sink, adequate fresh and gray water storage, and for everything to be stored at least four inches off the floor. The other aspect is safe food handling procedures, such as adequately washing your hands to avoid the spread of disease, food temperatures kept above 140 degrees or below 45 degrees, and appropriate procedures to avoid cross contamination of bacteria.

A few years ago, the food courts at most events looked like a hodgepodge of vagabond wagons. Not any more. Food concession booths must now comply structurally with increasingly more strict regulations in order to become licensed. And, as more information is learned about the science of food safety, they must also adhere to ever-more-strict food handling procedures. Until recently, most counties were able to implement their own food service regulations and policies within the guidelines of their state health department. This practice made food service and licensing complicated and confusing for concessionaires because health department regulations could vary from one county to the next. Now, however, many counties are required to adopt standard regulations as indicated by their state health department. This is good news for concessionaires. As we travel from county to county, we can be fairly certain we know, understand, and are in compliance with regulations. However, this may not be true in all areas of the country. Whereas some states may have standardized regulations for both structural and procedural elements of licensing, others may not. For this reason, do not plan your menu or booth or buy any equipment until you contact the governing county or state health departments where you plan to book your events. They will happily send you a handbook of regulations. Incidentally, the name of the department within the health department that deals with food service licensing changes from county to county. You may find them with Health and Human Services, or they may be hiding in The Department of Environmental Health.

Canadian Food Service Licensing

Across Canada, food service licensing is generally carried out by provincial governments, municipalities, or regional health authorities. For a list of each agency, refer to http://www.inspection.gc.ca/english/related/restaure.shtml for the Canadian Government website, with links to each agency.

In both the United States and Canada, the type of license and process of procuring a license for a temporary concession are very different from that of a permanent concession. It would be wise to understand the difference so that you can inquire into and acquire the license that is appropriate for your operation.

Permanent Concession Licensing

Mobile or Itinerant Permit

A food concession that plans to operate at a permanent location or a food truck that makes its daily rounds through industrial parks must be licensed with the health department as a mobile food unit. Sometimes called an "itinerant license," a mobile food unit is defined by the health department as a food service vehicle on wheels and is required to follow similar procedures for licensing as is a restaurant. Because of a mobile food unit's compact size, the additional procurement and licensing of a commissary or warehouse may be needed to meet maintenance and supply storage requirements. The steps of the process in your state may be:

1. Submit a plan review for the mobile food unit and a commissary or warehouse. Include a complete and detailed floor, plumbing, and electrical plan. You must also submit operational and logistical details of food handling and storage, toilet availability, fresh water source, gray water removal, and so on.

2. Wait for plan review denial or approval.

3. Resubmit plan with changes made as indicated.

4. Construct concession and commissary or warehouse.

5. Submit license application and fee.

6. Receive pre-opening inspection and approval.

Because of the strict structural requirements of a mobile food unit license, food booth tents and some pushcarts may be prohibited under this type of license. Additionally, a permanently located mobile food unit must also comply with all standard business licensing.

Commissaries and Warehouses

A mobile unit is generally too small to accommodate its own maintenance or to store all its necessary supplies and stock. Therefore, a licensed commissary or warehouse may also be needed to secure a license for the mobile unit. A commissary is a facility used to prepare food and to service the mobile food booth whereas a warehouse is a facility only used for the storage of extra supplies. Tools for cleaning, storage of food and supplies, water tank filling, gray water disposal, and an area for food preparation are all activities that may need to be performed in a separate facility to keep the food unit operational and within compliance. The type of extra facility (or facilities) you need is largely determined by the classification of your menu as determined by its degree of hazard to the public. In some cases, a health department will accept an arrangement you've made with the owner of a different licensed facility to perform your maintenance at his or her facility. For instance, you may get by with the written agreement from the owner of a neighborhood café, allowing you the use of his or her facility to service your food unit. Regulations may be written differently in your jurisdiction.

Temporary Concession Licensing

Temporary Restaurant Permit

Frequently, a new concessionaire is told he or she must have a mobile food unit license as well as a licensed commissary for his or her business. However, a food concession that sells food for a limited period of time at a specific temporary location is not required to be licensed as a *mobile food unit*, but rather as a *temporary restaurant*. A temporary restaurant license, commonly referred to as a "health permit," is issued by the county where the event is located and is good only for that single event. Compared to a *mobile food unit* license, this permit requires minimal structural requirements, does not need the additional licensing of a commissary, and is applicable to concession trailers, tents, and pushcarts. Additionally, a health permit is only required for booths that serve "potentially hazardous" food. A booth serving a "non-hazardous" menu, as defined by each local health department, may not require any licensing at all. This temporary permit is the health department's tool for monitoring the activities of transient or temporary enterprises, such as carnival food joints, nonprofit fundraisers, and concessionaires who bounce from community to community.

Most professional concessionaires don't prepare food in advance, but instead prepare all of their food in the concession while at the event. If they did prepare food in advance, they would need to have a licensed commissary or arrange for the use of a different licensed facility such as a local café or a church kitchen. Believe it or not, in some jurisdictions, nonprofit concessions get an additional third option. They are simply allowed to inform the public that the food was prepared in an unlicensed facility. For example, a nonprofit concession selling homemade pies can instead post a sign in the booth informing the public that the pies were baked at home. The pies are indeed authentically homemade.

Where allowed, concession trailer and pushcart operators may find it more economical to purchase instead a yearly *mobile food unit* license rather than a *temporary restaurant permit* for each event. As with any mobile food unit license, this license has a one-time yearly cost of $200 to $400 and is issued in the county of the operator's home base. As with a permanent concession, a health inspector will inspect and license the mobile food unit's "base of operation." The inspection includes the structural components of the mobile food unit, a commissary or warehouse facility, the water source, and the method of wastewater disposal. During the event season, the food handling aspects of the operation are then inspected on-site at each event for an additional small fee. Because concession tents aren't on wheels, they are not considered mobile food units and may not be allowed this option.

We all work in different parts of the country. When getting licensed in your area, you will find that any variances you experience from what I have described here are likely to be more about differ-

Though a temporary restaurant permit does not require the additional licensing of a commissary, most concessionaires have an extra (albeit unlicensed) facility nonetheless. Unless you live in a motor home and jump from event to event, you'll need a place to park your concession, and support vehicles between events. You'll likely also need a place to store stock, a freezer, supplies and extra equipment. A storage shed or garage is a handy place for cleaning and servicing all of your equipment.

ences in obtaining a mobile food unit license than a temporary restaurant permit. The reason being, a temporary health permit places emphasis on safe food handling procedure whereas, in addition to safe food handling procedure, a mobile food unit license places stronger emphasis on the structural aspects of the booth. Building codes, procedural policies, and regulations can be vastly different from bailiwick to bailiwick whereas procedures for maintaining food safety are universal.

> Here's a tip: Every aspect of your concession business will be impacted by your understanding of and ability to comply with health department regulations. Therefore, it is very important that you check with your county health department early in your planning to learn appropriate licensing requirements and procedures in your area.

Your Food Handler's Card

Food service workers are required to carry a food handler's card. This card is procured from any county health department and is good throughout the entire state. If you cross state lines, you will need to get a card for each state in which you work. The card is issued after successfully passing a multiple-choice quiz that tests your knowledge of safe food handling procedure. Most counties only require that at least one person with a food handlers card be on duty in the concession at all times. Rarely will they require everyone in the concession have a card.

As unpleasant as it may be to be scrutinized by the authorities everywhere you go, it is important to realize that it is extremely easy to make someone sick with food, particularly in the environment of a transient operation in the heat of summer. Health inspectors have an important job to do, so rather than become adversarial when they criticize your operation, be thankful that their scrutiny could save someone from suffering sickness or even death from eating your food.

Other Permits

From a national perspective, other forms of bureaucracy you may encounter might involve DBA (Doing Business As) business name registration, business licensing, federal identification number, state sales tax, state labor and industries, state and local fire marshals, and electrical inspections. One must assume that every area of the country might have some form of these types of local codes and ordinances. Additionally, there might be regional government offices in your area that have additional regulations you will also need to be aware of. Let's face it: The government loves its bureaucracy. You'll feel the love in some states more than others. The thing is, the food concession business falls into a kind of bureaucratic gray zone and in some instances operators can fly under the radar of some government agencies. I know some vendors who do everything they can to operate their business invisibly. I know as many others who operate strictly by the book. The best approach is to do your homework. Take the time to discover and educate yourself about every agency in your area that regulates your business activities.

Business Name Registration (DBA)

The state would like anyone who uses a business name other than his or her personal name to register it with the secretary of state's office. This business name is referred to as a DBA (Doing Business As). You do not need a business name to do business as a concession-aire. Therefore, you have several options. You could use your last name as your business name. Or you might want to think up a catchy name for your business but only use it on event applications to distinguish yourself from other vendors. Or you might decide to register your business name to establish a legal business identity. Many banks now require the registration of a DBA to open a business bank account. If you plan to set up accounts for credit with suppliers rather than to pay cash, you might want to validate your enterprise with a legal business name.

City or County Business Licensing

I'm sure if you were to walk into the city or county office and request a business license, they would be happy to sell you one. In actuality, without a business name and address, a temporary concession has no permanent location for which to be licensed. You might want to contact your county or city administrative offices for information on required business licensing in your area. Many communities require anyone who sells to or sees clients to be licensed even if the business is located somewhere else. For that reason, you may occasionally notice a business license application included with an event application. When this happens, the paperwork and cost is barely negligible and hardly worth mentioning.

Employer Identification Number (EIN)

The federal government issues an EIN, which is a nine-digit number assigned to businesses for tax filing and reporting purposes. If you hire employees, you are required to have an EIN. For information, publications, and forms for this or anything else involving the IRS (Internal Revenue Service), call 1/800-829-3676 or go to www.irs.gov.

State and Local Sales Tax

If you do events in one of the forty-five states with a state sales tax, you are responsible for collecting tax from your customers. Call the state department of revenue for a packet of instructions and an application, from which they will assign to you a tax-paying ID number.

State Labor and Industries

The state of Washington (and possibly other states, as well) has an obscure law that requires that food concession trailers be "stickered" for structural compliance with the Department of Labor and Industries. This is the state's way of ensuring that food booths meet the same codes for structural integrity that other commercially manufactured trailers must meet, thereby effectively discouraging people from slapping together a food trailer in their garage. This regulation does not affect nonresidents of the state, nor does it affect concession tents or stick joints. It is a poorly conceived and written law and has been disputed by the state courts.

All businesses that conduct business in the state of Washington and hire workers are required to register with the Department of Labor and Industries. The purpose is for reporting and paying workers' compensation insurance. If you live or work in Washington, contact www.wa.gov/insurance/employers.htm or call (360) 902-4817 for more information on this.

State Fire Marshal

The state fire marshal has a list of regulations pertaining to food concessions. Sometime the local fire marshal will visit your booth to make sure you have the appropriate type of fire extinguisher, your booth is not constructed of anything flammable, and your propane tanks are secure. Some states may additionally require a fire suppression hood or self-closing lid be installed over all equipment that uses combustible cooking oils. It has been my experience that frequently the fire marshal is only concerned that you have a good fire extinguisher. However, some fire marshals do inspect thoroughly and by the book and will not hesitate to shut down any booth that is not entirely compliant with state fire code. Be sure to call your state fire marshal for a list of the regulations that apply to food concessions in your state.

State Electrical Inspector

On occasion, while on-site to inspect the electrical affairs of the carnival, the state electrical inspector will also make the rounds to inspect the electric affairs of the food booths. In my experience, no permit or fees have been called for.

It is not uncommon to encounter the occasional overzealous government employee who interprets the law differently than you do. If you are armed with all the appropriate fire extinguishers, stickers, and permits, as well as a notebook of state administrative rules for all the pertinent agencies and departments that you may encounter, you will be well prepared to resolve any disputes. So far, the concession industry, being somewhat unconventional, has remained relatively unregulated. The downside is, it can be a little difficult to know for certain which regulations will apply. Sometimes we only learn of regulations when we are approached at an event by a public official. To be certain that doesn't happen you should have knowledge of every possible regulation that may apply to you. Find local agencies that deal with permits and taxes in your area by looking in the government pages of your phone book. Second, contact your secretary of state office for a free packet of information about business licensing and permits in your state. It also would be a good idea to interview some experienced vendors in your area. They are your best source for a straight answer.

Here's a tip: Small festivals are much more casual about enforcing regulations than are most fairs.

Insurance

Risk Management

Events can be dangerous places. They are crowded with distracted people, often poorly lit, and draped with tangled webs of electrical wires, hoses, and tent pegs. While attending an event, thousands of people may pet livestock, step unwashed out of portable toilets, and spend all afternoon spreading bacteria from one surface to the next where many more people can become exposed. Most people at an event are also served food from many different food booths, some of which have at least one worker who wasn't careful enough with safe food handling procedures. Someone is bound to get hurt! And when they do, someone is going to pay for it.

There are several things you can do to reduce your risk of losing everything to a lawsuit. First, you can make sure you do not have dangerous conditions around your booth for which you could be blamed. Be sure that propane bottles are secure, tent pegs are protected from toes, and that nothing sharp or hot is within reach of the public. Your booth will be swarming with people, some of whom will do things they shouldn't do and get into areas they have no business being in.

Many vendors create a privacy area behind their booths to prevent the public from getting into their work areas. A portable screen made by lashing a vinyl tarp within a PVC pipe frame is very effective at keeping the public out of your personal space.

Another step you can take to reduce your risk is to train your helpers in safe food handling procedures. Even if they are not required to carry a food handler's card, you may still want them to read the handbook for the education. You may also want to spend the extra time to follow up on and resolve any food handling bad habits that have developed.

Finally, whether your customer is afflicted with food poisoning, chokes on a piece of gristle, or trips over a tent peg, you want to be protected financially with business liability insurance. Since the E. coli outbreaks of the early 1990s, many events now require concessionaires to carry insurance with one million dollars in coverage. Not only is the insurance protection itself important, but also, in the event of a lawsuit, your insurance company attorneys are there to fight your case. Business liability insurance may be a wise purchase; however, it may not be necessary in your area. In the Pacific Northwest, only about half of all events require it, and many vendors are able to find enough events to keep busy without purchasing insurance.

General Liability Insurance

A general business liability policy covers two areas of risk: claims against your premises and claims against your product. New concessionaires often find it difficult to find liability coverage for their business. There are a limited number of companies that offer coverage to "mobile food services," and for those, the premiums are usually very high. As with any business, preferred insurance providers want to insure a business with a sound track record. However, in some cases, they may accept new concessionaires with previous experience through some other capacity. Running a restaurant, managing a concession for someone else, or working in a restaurant, as well as managing an unrelated business, may all be considered adequate evidence of experience.

Concessionaires would like an insurance agent who provides good customer service. Unlike other businesses, we must frequently provide a "certificate of insurance" specifically naming the event as "additionally insured." Not all insurance agencies are willing to provide this type of extra customer service.

General liability insurance does not cover your business assets. By nature, the concession business must depart from the address of the insured in order to conduct business. This departure is what prevents the policy from covering the assets. Though the risk to equipment is higher while you are traveling to and from or while you are attending an event, if the damage occurs while the equipment is associated with your vehicle, it will be covered by your auto insurance policy.

Vehicle Liability Insurance

Concessionaires travel great distances in their vehicles, stocking up on supplies and getting from one event to the next. As with any motorized vehicle on the road, each one must be protected with liability insurance. Regular vehicle coverage extends from the vehicle to any unit it is towing. For example, if you happen to smash into someone's booth with your trailer while you are backing into your space, your policy will cover it. However, unless you specifically have a business policy, when your insurance company learns that your trailer is used to conduct business, it may subsequently cancel your policy.

CHAPTER 4

What's to Eat?
Planning Your Menu

Operational Considerations of Your Menu

Designing your menu should be your first consideration when planning your concession business. Other planning, such as booth design, vehicle requirements, equipment, licensing, events, and helpers, will all be directly related to your menu. The list of possible menu items is endless. We are all familiar with the standard fair foods like hamburgers, hot dogs, corn dogs, ice cream, pie, corn on the cob, cotton candy, candied apples, curly fries, elephant ears, snow cones, and kettle corn. And there are also more elaborate dishes, such as Asian food, fajitas, burritos, fish and chips, pizza, meatballs, sausage and onions, and Philly steak sandwiches. The list of possible menu items is endless. Some vendors sell traditional fair food while others concoct their own special dishes.

If you are like most concessionaires, the menu you start with will not be the menu you stick with. Concessionaires are constantly looking for new menu ideas. They would like a menu that sells well, is easily prepared, has a high profit margin, and has little competition. They also look for something that does not drive them nuts with logistical difficulties such as extensive preparation time and excessive waste. There is no such thing as a perfect menu. Every aspect of a menu, both good and bad, is a trade-off for a different aspect. The trick is to realize each of those aspects and then prioritize them. For example, it is likely that a menu item that is easy to prepare has a low profit margin. A dish that serves up quickly likely requires extensive preparation time. And a menu that has many good aspects is one that is already being sold by everyone else. So, how do you decide which menu is right for you? I recommend that you start with a list. Whether you spend time thinking of different menu ideas or already have plans to sell your world's greatest duck tail tacos, it is important to itemize, dissect, and analyze every detail of every aspect of that menu. Your list of potential dishes and their associated ingredients and supplies, as well as their handling, preparation, and storage considerations will guide your thinking toward determining the menu that is best for you. Many closely related considerations, such as equipment, booth design, and vehicles will be addressed in detail later.

Consider the following generalizations. When analyzing your ideas, these generalizations may or may not apply to your menu. Some menus fall into more than one category.

- *Dishes that are pre-cooked or pre-prepared* for your customers serve quickly, which maximizes sales during a rush. However, they may require extensive pre-preparation of ingredients either prior to opening or as needed during the day. Often the ingredients, once prepped and/or cooked, are wasted if not sold. The quality and safety of products that are pre-prepped or pre-cooked must be maintained during slow periods. Most products that are cooked on a grill have some element of pre-prep to them. Pre-prep items include: Asian food, fajitas, sausage and onions, cotton candy, and most meat dishes.

- *Dishes that are cooked or prepared to order* take longer to prepare and serve, restricting sales during a rush. Quality of product is easy to maintain because everything is served fresh. The public hates to wait, but loves to watch you prepare food. Some items may still require some pre-prep. Items prepared on the spot include: curly fries, elephant ears, hamburgers, espresso, and shaved ice.

- *Popular, easy-to-sell dishes* are so common that getting bookings into many events is difficult because event coordinators often restrict the duplication of menus. If you do get into an event with this kind of menu, the competition will be fierce. Particularly popular items include: corn dogs, curly fries, hamburgers, and hot dogs.

- *Some popular items may be restricted* by an exclusive right to sell contract clause, referred to as an "X," which the carnival may have with the event. Commonly restricted items include: cotton candy, caramel and candy apples, and pronto pups (corn dogs).

- *Popular dishes* that are commonly sold by nonprofit organizations are often difficult to get into an event because the event may provide the nonprofits with an "X." If you do get in, nonprofits nearly always price their menu much lower than market value, making them very difficult to compete with. Common favorites sold by nonprofits include: hamburgers, hot dogs, pie, and chicken barbecue.

- *Items that are pre-processed* are very quick and easy to prepare and serve but are generally costly, which greatly reduces your profit margin. Pre-processed items include: pizza, hot pockets, onion rings, and poppers.

- *Dishes containing a lot of meat* are usually popular but are costly, which means your "high-ticket" menu may reduce your sales in communities with a slow economy. Also, meat dishes are generally more preferred by adults than kids and therefore reduce the size of your market.

- *Unique menus* such as ethnic and vegetarian foods may be hard to sell if customers do not understand what it is they are buying. This is especially true away from diversely populated communities. However, if your target market is ethnic or bohemian—and assuming you can find enough of these types of events—you may be very successful.

- *Common fair food* such as pronto pups may be hard to sell at events with a demographic that is health conscious and has discriminating taste.

- *Many popular dishes are time-sensitive* meaning they may only sell well on a hot day, a cold day, or after dinner. Some of these items include: ice cream, shaved ice, chili, hot chocolate, coffee, and desserts.

- *Regionally popular dishes may not sell well outside of that particular region.* For example, gumbo may not sell well in the Northwest.

Some vendors try to maximize the positive while they reduce the negative aspects of a menu. Some common ways of doing this are:

- *Focus on a menu item that is somewhat unique* but not unknown and may be considered an old favorite.

- *Present a new twist to an old favorite.* By making a common dish unique, event booking opportunities can be increased. Customers get bored with regular fair food but are intrigued by something that is new but not scarily new.

- *Make a dish from scratch.* This usually reduces its cost and improves its quality.

- *Bulk up a meat dish* by adding inexpensive filler such as rice or noodles.

- *Sell large volumes of product.* By applying the principle of economy of scale, labor and product costs are reduced.

- *Charge a healthy price based on value.* Good food deserves a good return.

No matter how you slice it, all menus have their faults. It's also important to point out that no menu sells well all of the time, nor at every event. Many other variables besides quality of menu play a factor in sales. Once you establish a successful menu that works well for you most of the time, stick with it. Allow it a chance to develop a following and become established as "your menu" with event coordinators and the public.

Almost all menus are cyclical. Some menus are trendy. Within a space of five years a dish can go from being completely unknown and unpopular to being on every event's bestseller list. Vendors from all around jump on the new menu bandwagon. When it soon becomes over-booked at every event, vendors scramble to drop it from their menu to make room for the next new big seller.

Espresso coffee wasn't popular at first. Now it is. The best thing about the espresso craze is that it ushered in all sorts of other specialty beverages. Five years ago, no beverage would sell for more than two dollars. Now, vendors expect to get three to four dollars for almost any drink. Not only did this new craze broaden the beverage market, but it also elevated the status (and price) of all top-quality dishes. The timing couldn't have been better. With the price of fuel, space fees, and everything else going up, vendors were really struggling to hold onto their margins.

Espresso served from a small manufactured trailer.

Here are some other tips for planning your menu:

Many vendors expand their menu by being creative with their standard ingredients and equipment. For instance, the ingredients and equipment used to make burritos can also be used to make tacos, taco salads, and quesadillas. By presenting a variation of these same ingredients the menu grows from one item to four. Taking that concept further, you can create a variation on a common item that can set your menu apart. For example, chicken teriyaki stir-fry is a very common and popular dish in this area. A vendor might add pineapple, call it Hawaiian stir-fry, and now has a different menu than his neighbor. With this kind of creative thinking the possibilities are limitless and so are the benefits.

A menu that has at least one unique and impressive dish is much easier to book into events. Event coordinators are always looking for a well-balanced assortment of menus for the benefit of their attendees. Many coordinators also have a policy of limiting duplication of menus for the benefit of vendors. By adding just one unique but impressive item to your menu and promoting your business on that dish you greatly improve your odds of being offered a space in an event. This is true even if you secretly assume that the bulk of your sales will be on the balance of your common, but more profitable standard menu. For instance, by promoting your world's greatest meatball sandwich you easily book into events, but your hot dogs and pop may in actuality make up the majority of your sales.

Vendors who are willing to diversify their menus by selling any of several different menu options will increase their chance of being offered a contract. Frequently, vendors will be offered a space at an event, but not with the usual menu they offer. By being flexible enough to offer a different menu they will secure their contract.

The saying "time is money" is no truer anywhere than it is in a food booth. Actually, "seconds count" is a more accurate statement. Whatever you sell, it is critical that it should either be prepared in advance of sales or prepared quickly to order. Concessionaires have a very limited window of time to make sales and cannot afford to require their customers to wait more than three minutes to receive their food. Further, they should also be capable of serving or preparing food for more than one customer at a time. Imagine the difference in sales between two hamburger booths. In one, a single person methodically cooks and assembles a hamburger one at a time for each customer. In the other, the grill is loaded with twenty-four hamburger patties as two people assemble and serve.

Consider the labor involved in making and serving your menu. Labor will impact how quickly you can serve your product and/or how many helpers will be needed to get the food quickly to your customers. Using hamburgers again as an example, count the number of minutes, steps, and procedures from getting patties on the grill to the finished hamburger in the customer's hand. Compare that to the number of minutes, steps, and procedures in dipping an ice cream cone.

Some dishes are more economical when made from scratch. Onion rings, for example, have a much higher profit margin when sliced fresh onion is dipped in batter and fried than when purchased frozen, pre-sliced, and battered. Additionally, pre-processed frozen inventory is much harder to manage than fresh. Frozen product requires a lot of freezer space. Fresh onion rings only require bags of onions and some boxes of dry batter. On the other hand, some dishes are not more economical when made from scratch. Lemonade made from a "Country Time" mix costs pennies per serving compared to scratch lemonade made with lemon juice and sugar. In either case, labor is nearly always more involved when a dish is made from scratch.

Consider the weight of the equipment needed for your menu. If you are a one-person tent operation, you may have a tough time maneuvering a four-foot grill that weighs several hundred pounds. The accumulation of heavy equipment can also overload a small trailer.

No matter what type or size of menu you choose, your sales objective should always be focused on volume. Make all of your related plans for equipment, vehicles, storage, inventory, and staff around that goal. If you plan and equip your menu to dabble with a mere one hundred sales per day, your equipment, stock on hand, or available helpers will not be prepared when the rush hits, and you will lose your chance to cover your event costs, much less make any money.

It is wise to consider the overall cost of serving your menu. Aside from the cost of each product that goes into a serving, there are other costs to consider as well. For example, a deep fried menu also has the additional cost of propane for deep fryers, frying oil, and buckets of ketchup. And, as we saw in the example of serving hamburgers, some menus also require a larger staff. When calculating profit margin and pricing, be sure to plug into the formula a cost for these expenses as well.

Planning the Best Menu for High Profit

There are three important elements you should consider when deciding on a menu—logistics, profit margin, and popularity.

Logistics: The logistics of a menu can be complex. How much time does it take to prepare? How many people does it take to prepare and serve without holding up sales? How much and what type of storage or freezer space does each product on the menu require? Will it spoil quickly or can unsold product be carried to the next event? Can each product be purchased easily or must it be special ordered? The big question here is: Is your menu one that can be easily prepared en masse? And can it withstand the ordeals of storage and transportation? It is one thing to serve a dish successfully to fifty people at the family reunion and quite another to serve a dish day in and out to thousands of people from a transient operation.

> Unless you have unlimited helpers, a menu that requires the fewest number of people to prepare and serve is best. Hiring help costs money and causes your business to depend on the dependability of others.

Profit Margin: The profit margin is simple to calculate by dividing the selling price into the cost of each serving. If the margin is not adequate for your business, you can possibly adjust your dish to make it less expensive to serve. Or you can raise the price. Some dishes may not work out. Depending on your venues and customer base, high-priced dishes may never sell well enough.

Popularity: What you sell must be desirable enough that people make a conscious decision to stand in line waiting to have it. Menus that only spark impulse purchases will never make enough money. That's the litmus test. That's not to say there should be a line at your booth all the time or at every event. Generally, if there are lines of customers at other booths, there should be a line at your booth as well. If your booth doesn't generate substantial interest, there is a reason for it. Do some troubleshooting. Are your signs adequate? If not, improve them. Is your dish too unusual? If so, hand out samples. Are your prices too high? Lower them. A good way to get some insight into the reason for the slow sales is to ask your customers what they think. Although most people are hesitant to provide constructive criticism to a stranger, some will if you ask for their honesty. Their input could be helpful. Ask if the food is okay or how it could be improved. Maybe the service counter is too high or the booth is the wrong color. You may be surprised by what you learn.

If you have done everything you can to encourage business but your menu still can't rally sales, you may want to change your menu. Let's face it: Some menus aren't popular. There comes a point for many of us when we have to quit making excuses. Perhaps at one event the weather is too hot. At another we have a bad space location. At another our menu is duplicated. Something always causes sales to suffer. Unfortunately, there is no such thing as a perfect event, and there is definitely no such thing as a whole season of perfect events. Your menu and entire operation must be able to rise above anything and everything that impedes sales. The sooner you quit making excuses for your menu or booth and get down to correcting each and every possible problem, the more money you will make.

Think carefully about your menu. Your world will revolve around the food you serve, as will your bank account. Fortunately, if you are unhappy with either, you can change

Here's a tip: If you are still stumped for ideas for a good menu, try watching cable TV shows about fast food. These shows take you to locally or regionally famous fast food joints around the country that sell outlandish dishes.

your menu. The problem is, in no time at all your business will become associated with your menu in the minds of event coordinators and your customers. By changing it, you risk alienating both. You will possibly have to start over in establishing your business by finding new events and creating a following of customers for your new menu. On the other hand, tweaking your menu can be a good thing. Don't be afraid to experiment with new ideas. An addition or variation to your menu can change the dynamic of your whole operation, resulting in possibly a need for hiring more help and/or investing in bigger equipment or more storage capacity. But the change may also bring more business to your booth, cause your operation to become more efficient, or get you a contract at a bigger and better event.

Above all else, your menu should be determined by your goals. If you want a concession business that will be easy to operate and provide you with extra spending money, you can set yourself up fairly simply with a small, easy menu. However, if your plan is ultimately to earn a living from your concession, you will need to generate substantial cash flow by gearing your menu toward high-ticket, high-volume items. It is important to remember that many of the costs of doing business, such as your space fees, travel costs,

Here's a tip: I know one new vendor who was very excited to start his business selling a special dish that was fabulously delicious. He learned very quickly that he had underestimated the importance of accounting for lengthy preparation time. Because his dish took one full day to purchase and portion, and a second day to marinate, he didn't have enough time between events to prepare and stock up. Also, because of his menu's lengthy prep time, he had no hope of rapidly replenishing his stock once depleted from a rush. After making adjustments and finding ways to speed up the preparation of his menu, he was eventually very successful.

health permits, liability insurance, personnel expenses, and investment of time will be roughly the same no matter your menu. What this means is: You would need to sell twice as many $2 bags of ho-hos as $4 piggy pops to cover your expenses and show a profit. Large operations that sell thousands of five and six dollar orders generate the cash flow that is necessary to invest in the necessities of a high-volume operation, such as a large staff of helpers, newer and larger vehicles, high capacity equipment, and working capital. They can also afford the steep percentage space fees that are charged at the high attendance events, which they must attend to produce the high grossing sales figures. In short, by achieving critical mass, they are hugely profitable. Whatever your ambitions, it is important to achieve the right balance in your operation between what is logistically achievable for you, with a menu that sells well enough for you to meet your particular goal

Curly fries, corn dog, and two flavors of lemonade.

Broaden Your Market with Menu Variety

Along with everything else, you should also consider how large your menu should be. Some vendors believe that it is a benefit to have something to offer everyone in the family. They offer food for mom, dad, and the kids, as well as a beverage. It is a fact that many families understandably do not want to stand in more than one line to get everything they need. On this subject there are two theories: more is better and less is better. The folks in the "more is better" camp believe that the more you have to offer, the more customers you will have. This is true, but may or may not be an advantage. A large menu is definitely an advantage when business is slow because it broadens your appeal to your customers and creates additional revenue. On the other hand, a lengthy menu of nuisance items is a liability during a rush when your customers are holding up your line because they can't decide what to order for each and every indecisive member of the family.

Even if your single-dish menu sells well enough, you may want to put your eggs into more than one basket. Carefully diversifying your menu is a good way to provide insurance in case your main dish bombs. In addition to broadening your market, a diversified menu protects you from common catastrophes such as excessive duplication of menus and inappropriate weather for your dish. Better still, the correct combination of multiple items can compound sales. Each person who orders may buy several complementary items and put a twenty-dollar bill in your till rather than a five. It's an easy sale to make with nine easy words, "Can I get you a _____ with that _____?" Some vendors have a large variety of dishes available until a rush hits. Then the items on their menus that are slow to prepare or have a low profit margin get marked as "sold out" on the menu boards until the rush is over.

Other related factors worthy of consideration are the size of your supply shopping list and the time and effort it takes to stock up. A single-dish menu may have a shopping list of six ingredients and associated serving products whereas a menu of four items may require a shopping list of thirty or more assorted products. The time, energy, and space for hauling and storing all of these products should also be considered.

Beverages for Added Value

A few years ago, nearly all food vendors sold soda pop. At that time it was by far the most popular beverage and, on a hot summer day, the most popular item on anyone's menu. Now, however, although pop still sells well, many vendors have switched to or added a large assortment of bottled waters, juices, and gourmet bottled specialty drinks.

With the increased availability and popularity of a large variety of bottled beverages, many vendors buy cases of product from their soda pop distributor, Costco or their local Cash and Carry wholesale grocer. At the event, they simply display the bottles in a large ice chest placed on the ground in front of their booth. Naturally, the cooler lid is open so the customers can't miss the frosty cold bottles cradled in ice. This technique saves them from buying, storing, and hauling sleeves of cups, lids, straws, and enough ice for every cup of pop they sell.

Soda Pop

Dispensable soda pop is sold in two ways, pre-mix and post-mix.

Pre-mix is pre-mixed by the bottling company and is the same beverage you get when you drink pop from a bottle or can. The soda pop in each five-gallon pre-mix canister is pushed through the dispenser with CO_2 gas dispensed from a five-gallon tank. The dispenser is chilled with either ice or electricity so the pop will dispense without foaming.

Post-mix, on the other hand, is syrup dispensed from a carton. The syrup is mixed with water as it flows through the dispenser. Permanent concessions and restaurants with plumbed water prefer to use post-mix because it costs less and takes up less space. Temporary concessions cannot depend on the availability or quality of water at each event and therefore prefer to sell pre-mix.

Soda pop companies such as Pepsi and Coca Cola are very generous (in exchange for your business) about supplying vendors with everything they need to set up and sell their products. With a phone call to your local pop distributor, they will provide you with a list of all the products and equipment they offer, as well as a product cost analysis sheet. Most large events are sponsored by a specific soda pop company. The company naturally requires all the participating vendors to sell exclusively their product. At these events, they will happily deliver to you a pop dispenser (on loan, free of charge), CO_2 tank, as many five-gallon tanks of pre-mix product that you need, as well as ice, cups, and lids. They will also offer cases of bottled product. If you ask, they will include a free menu board and a custom lettered banner for advertising. Delivery is usually made the day before the event. During the event they will come around each morning to inquire if you need anything more. When the event ends, they will return to pick up borrowed equipment, empty tanks, unopened product, and settle the bill. Generally, their policy is to collect payment for your entire order when they deliver it. When the show ends, they will credit you for what you didn't open. The problem to be aware of is: If you tear down and leave the event before they arrive to settle up, you may not get your credit. Be sure to ask about their delivery/pickup schedule when you place your order. Many pop distributors will offer this same service even at smaller non-sponsored events. If they don't deliver to an event, you can pick up what you need at their distribu-

Here's a tip: Some areas of the country are frequently sponsored by Pepsi whereas others are more frequently sponsored by Coke. Because each company uses dispensers with unique fittings, if you plan to install your own pop dispenser in your booth, you may want to line yourself up with the company that most frequently sponsors events in your area. This will prevent you from needing to switch back and forth frequently between dispensers and product.

tion warehouse. Steady customers will often be supplied with a pop dispenser on loan for the season.

Offering a beverage on your menu does increase your gross sales, particularly when the weather is hot. Because handling and transporting all of the components of pop service taxes operations resources, many vendors only serve pop when they are working at pop-sponsored events. At sponsored events, everything they need is delivered to the site and picked up at the event's closing.

Condiments

Most dishes are improved by a dollop of sauce or salt. Additionally, your customers will appreciate the easy availability of a napkin and straw. Concessionaires sometimes put these types of items on the front counter in easy reach of the booth worker to be easily refilled as needed. Others put them on a small side table, away from the front counter, so the customers can take their time doctoring their food without holding up the line. Whatever arrangement you make for your condiments, keep in mind that the health department will expect them to be kept sanitary and safe from spoilage. Sauces are frequently dispensed from pump canisters. Aside from being tidy, they are far more economical. Single serving packets are expensive and can create a huge litter problem.

I find condiments to be a source of irritation. I blame fast food restaurants for corrupting the public's sense of "condiment etiquette." My temperature goes up when someone buys food from my neighbor, then walks over to my booth where they help themselves to my condiments. I nearly simmer when customers take far more napkins or ketchup than they could possibly need. I have a stroke when the two events occur at once! When that happens, I try to remind myself that just as frequently, my neighboring vendors are angry with my customers for the same reasons.

A custom built nonprofit booth with the condiment table placed away from the service window.

Selecting Suppliers

From the start, your supplier is a valuable source of important information in planning your business. This information is used to determine precisely what you will sell, what price you will charge, the equipment you'll need, and the operational logistics you'll encounter in food storage, transport, and handling. In turn, these decisions will have an impact on every other component of your business. With a notebook, calculator, and shopping list, make a trip to your local Cash and Carry wholesale grocer. For each product on your list—menu ingredients, condiments, and paper products—jot down the unit and case price, product size, and package dimensions. Also explore the choices in selection of a variety of products. Some products are available as fresh, frozen, canned, dried, refrigerated, pre-processed, or pre-portioned. Precisely determining your stock and supplies based on cost, handling, and transport considerations, as well as the quality and appropriateness to your menu and operation, can be a complicated process. Keep a ledger of the breakdown in cost per serving of each item on your list. You will refer to it frequently to stay abreast of profit margins and price setting. You need to know how many servings you will get from a unit of product to calculate portion sizes, prices, and amount of stock to bring to an event to satisfy targeted sales. The package size and dimensions are initially important in planning your food handling, storage, equipment, and transport needs. Further, knowing how many cases of product will fit into a freezer or ice chest and how much weight and shelf space your product requires has an influence on the type of booth, support vehicles, and the size of your staff.

Once your business is in operation, stocking up on supplies will become an important and time-consuming part of management. You want the task to be performed as efficiently as possible. Most vendors have a storage facility at or near their homes. They stock up on supplies before the event by making a trip or two to Costco or their local Cash and Carry wholesale grocer. With lots of storage and freezer space, they have a convenient place to store their stock until they go to an event. Some vendors have their supplies delivered to their facility by a wholesale grocer. Vendors who work large fairs often have their product and supplies delivered directly to an event. Neither Costco nor Cash and Carry offers a delivery service, but their prices are lower than the many wholesalers who do. Sometimes vendors will have large, heavy, or difficult-to-purchase items delivered to their facilities by one supplier whereas they purchase the easy-to-manage products from Costco or Cash and Carry. Don't be afraid to shop around to find the best prices and product for your menu. For example, a vendor who uses diced chicken thigh might find a lower price and a more precise-sized dice for his or her menu by shopping wholesale meat suppliers or butchers than could otherwise be obtained from a wholesale grocer. Custom orders can be supplied in a appropriate package size to suit your handling and portioning needs. A custom order might also be purchased in your choice of package size and weight to accommodate better your storage and freezer dimensions.

Incidentally, the health department insists that everything you serve be acquired from an approved source. You are not allowed to serve to the public the clams you dug at the beach, the venison you shot and butchered, or the wild mushrooms you harvested yourself. You get the point.

Performing a Product Cost Analysis

Once you have come up with an idea or ideas for your menu, you will need to calculate the cost of each serving of each item on your menu. These calculations will let you know if your menu has potential for profit, as well as determine your selling price. By breaking down the cost of each ingredient (and paper) into the cost of each serving and dividing that number by your selling price, you will know the cost of product and profit margin for each item. Concessionaires like to have an average cost of product at less than 23 percent. Stated another way, they like to have a 77 percent profit margin. There are some product costs, such as that for deep fry oil, ice, or wasted product that cannot be easily calculated into each serving. Because of these hard-to-calculate costs, your cost analysis will likely ultimately reflect "cost of goods" at 25 percent. For example, a cost analysis for a hot dog may look like this:

One ¼ lb. all-beef dog	$ .92
One hot dog bun	.23
One serving tissue	.01
One pickle slice	.02
One serving condiments	.01
	$1.19
Proposed selling price:	$3.25

Total cost of product divided by selling price: 1.19/3.25 = .36

Cost of product per serving at .36 (36 percent) is too high. In this case, a vendor could shop for less expensive dogs and buns and raise the selling price. Perhaps by switching to "all-meat" dogs, finding a less expensive source for buns, and raising the price to $3.75, the vendor could change the equation to:

One ¼ lb. all-meat dog	$ .77
One hot dog bun	.14
One serving tissue	.01
One pickle slice	.02
One serving condiments	.01
	$.95
Proposed selling price:	$3.75

Total cost of product divided by selling price: .95/3.75 = .25

With a little pencil sharpening, the cost and price for a serving of hot dog can be brought to a 75 percent profit margin and within the range of profitability. Seventy-five percent! Ka-ching, you may be thinking. Though that may sound like a huge profit margin, it's not. When you factor into the equation the additional 25 percent for overhead

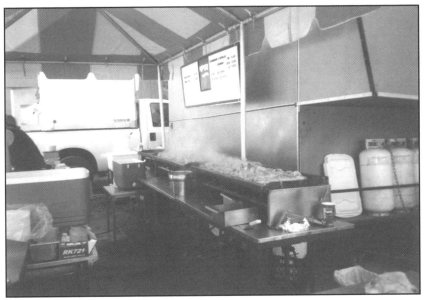

Inside a pole tent are two 4' homemade grills loaded with cooking product. The grills are setting on homemade folding tables covered with stainless steel. Notice the propane tanks mounted on the home-made stock trailer, all conveniently accessible along the back wall of the tent.

costs and the more consequential component of seasonality, a concession business requires something near a 75 percent margin to stay in business. Like farming, your booth must earn enough during a short season to pay the bills all year.

Cost Analysis

Ingredient	per unit	per each	per serving menu item Corn Dogs	per serving menu item Hot Dogs	per serving menu item #3	per serving menu item #4	per serving menu item #5
corn dog/72cs	21.52	0.3	0.3				
fry oil/5gal	17.51		0.01				
ketchup/6cs	16.42	2.74	0.05	0.05			
serving tissue/1000	11.45	0.011	0.011	0.011			
wieners/10lb	36.80	0.92		0.92			
buns/24cs	5.76	0.24		0.24			
Total			0.37	1.22			
Cost per/serving			0.37	1.22			
			Menu corn dog	Menu hot dog	Menu Item #3	Menu Item #4	Menu Item #5
Selling Price			2.00	3.75			
Product Cost			0.37	1.22			
Net Profit			1.63	2.53			
% (cost/price)			0.19	0.33			

Performing a cost analysis of each ingredient and paper product per serving is crucial for tracking costs and setting prices.

Part 2

Planning Your Booth and Equipment

CHAPTER 5

Designing, Buying, or Building Your Food Booth

Choosing the Right Booth for You

Designing your food booth is the most exciting aspect of starting a concession business, as well as the most involved. Booths come in limitless variations, ranges of sophistication, and prices. It is with the design of our booth that we express our individuality and distinguish ourselves to the public and to our peers. In fact, our identity is so entwined with our food booths that we refer to each other as booths. For example, while gossiping, one vendor might say to another, "That booth down there, they don't know...." I know it's poor grammar. But it's just the way it is.

A concession booth must meet all of the licensing requirements of the health department and any other pertinent governing agencies, as well as enable you to serve quality food to thousands of customers in a very short period of time. Your booth is also the place you'll call home for much of the season.

Almost all food booths fall into one of five categories: trailer, tent, stick joint, motorized van, or pushcart. However, occasionally you may see a concession that is unique and can't be classified. Like everything else in this business, there are advantages and disadvantages to each type of booth. Before you shop for a booth, you should have a good idea what your menu and associated equipment will be, as well as the type of events you plan to work.

Certain types of booths are more appropriate for certain types of menus, venues, and the size of operation you plan to have. A concessionaire who plans to work small, quick events such as parades, ball games, and auctions would not be happy with a large pole tent that takes hours to set up. He or she might want a booth that is self-contained with its own water tank and electric generator. The more self-contained a booth is, the more events become available. A small, quick booth might also be set up with a menu that requires the fewest number of people to operate. Sales in a small booth may be limited, but you can make up for that with the increased availability of venues and lower operating costs.

A small, custom-built trailer with a simple menu.

Vendors who plan to do large, high-volume fairs need a booth that provides enough room for all the equipment, stock, and workers to get the job done. Sometimes this means having a large trailer or pole tent as well as a support vehicle parked near or behind the booth.

Many large operations have an awning, extra tent, or support vehicle off the back of the booth where freezers, ice machines, ice chests, and work tables can be used for preparing or storing product. Also, these large operations often use more water than their water tanks can hold and need to run a water hose to the booth, either temporarily to fill the tank or as a constant source of water. Any time a concessionaire asks for extra amenities such as these they diminish their appeal to event coordinators and risk not getting booth space simply because the event can't provide for the extra needs of the booth. The extra labor, time, and money it takes to operate a large booth can also limit the desirability of certain events, reducing the number of possible events to choose from and apply for.

If you're considering contracting with a carnival to sell on the carnival midway, you would want a booth that is visually appealing and accessible to the public on all sides. A booth with piles of extra stock scattered around the outside would create a hazard to carnival goers.

A manufactured concession on the carnival midway.

Further, concessionaires with physical limitations would likely be happier with a trailer because it is easier to set up and operate.

Although these are all important considerations, the type of food booth a concessionaire uses mostly comes down to personal preference. No matter what booth type you choose, it must be able to withstand a heavy beating. Over the course of the season, heavy stock and equipment gets repeatedly loaded in and out of your trailer or truck. While being driven down the road, plenty of things will fall over and be broken. All of your stuff will either be spilled or get spilled on. By the end of the season, everything will be dented, cracked, and covered in grime. Hired help is rarely as careful with your equipment as you are. Be sure to plan for this rough treatment when designing or purchasing your booth and all of the equipment that goes in it.

Concession Trailers

A concession trailer is a kitchen on wheels. Conveniently contained within a 7' wide by 10' to 30' long box are all the necessities of your operation. Most trailers have, at the very least, a plumbed three-compartment sink and hand washing sink, a fresh and gray water storage tank system, electrical system, food preparation equipment, and miscellaneous supplies.

Concession trailers have many advantages over other types of booths. They are fully equipped and easy to clean and maintain. They offer protection from the weather, which is very important in windy or rainy regions of the country. And they are easily locked for security. On the other hand, trailers have some serious disadvantages as well. They have limited space for equipment and workers, which has a large impact on sales capacity. Also, because they are enclosed, with small service windows and high counters, the public finds them less assessable. In fact, most vendors will tell you that when all else is equal, most customers would prefer to buy from a tent than a trailer. There may be other reasons for this bias aside from accessibility. Many trailers are one-dimensional when viewed from the midway or frequently lack an eye-catching display with which to attract business. With heat-producing appliances on the inside and the sun beating down on the outside, they can additionally become uncomfortable when you spend all day inside working. On the other hand, when the weather is cold or windy, a trailer is a much more comfortable place to work than booths that are exposed to the elements.

The service window is one of the most important components of the trailer. Ideally, it should be big enough that the public can easily see what's going on inside, as well as allow you to see easily what's going on outside. What you see through the window will be the only view you have for the duration of the event. Concessionaires rapidly grow to despise their trailer if it's claustrophobic. The service window should also be low enough so that curious kids can easily see inside without trying to elevate themselves by doing pull-ups on the side of your trailer. Most trailers are built with the floor approximately 15" off of the ground. At that height, a service window that is cut low enough for the public to see in is too low for the server to comfortably serve out. Many custom-manufactured concession trailers are built on a "drop axle," enabling the floor between the wheel wells to be much lower than it otherwise would be on a straight axle. It is much easier to take orders and money and to hand out the food when the concessionaire stands at or near the same level as the customers.

Most trailers have a window flap/awning over the service window, which is pulled up and braced to provide a small roof over the people standing at your window. The flap protects your front counter and your customers from the weather. It also adds vital visual appeal by creating visual depth to the trailer. However, the awning can be a sales liability. Some events require every component of your booth to be placed behind the frontage line. At these events, a booth with a large awning will set well back from its non-awning neighbor, losing vital visibility. There should also be ample floor space to allow all the workers inside to move through their assigned tasks without stepping over and on each other.

If you choose a concession trailer as your food booth, there is more to consider. Many events are crowded with booths, buildings, telephone poles, and other obstacles and require careful maneuvering (usually backward, in reverse gear) to position the trailer into its assigned space. A hitch that is long enough to allow the trailer and tow vehicle to jackknife as needed will prevent you from smashing the front corner of the trailer on the rear corner of the vehicle. A small, single-axle trailer will maneuver much more easily than will a long dual-axle trailer. On the other hand, while going down the highway, a dual-axle trailer loaded with heavy restaurant equipment is not only more stable but is also much safer than one with a single axle. Each standard trailer axle is designed to handle only 3,500 pounds of weight. Additionally, in the case of a blowout, it is reassuring to know that, with a dual-axle trailer, the three remaining tires will probably get you to the exit ramp whereas the one remaining tire on a single-axle trailer definitely will not.

Another consideration is the gross weight of the trailer in relation to the size of the tow vehicle. Trailers are heavy once loaded with heavy restaurant equipment and stock. The gross weight of your tow vehicle should be substantially more than the gross weight of the trailer. Also, if the gross weight of your trailer is over 6,500 pounds, a standard-size pickup truck might not have the braking and pulling capacity to handle every driving situation safely.

When you design the interior for equipment, be sure to balance your weight from side to side and front to back. An extra two hundred pounds of tongue weight will keep the trailer pulling smoothly without bobbing up and down like a seesaw or wagging back and forth like a fishtail. Aside from better weight distribution, if the trailer doesn't pull smoothly, the installation of load levelers and/or sway bars can help remedy the problem.

Most people get a concession trailer by either purchasing a new, unequipped manufactured concession trailer, custom build one from the ground up, convert an RV or other vehicle into a concession, or purchase one of the above, used and pre-equipped from another vendor.

Manufactured Concession Trailers

Manufactured trailers are becoming increasingly more popular, particularly in areas with stringent licensing regulations. There are many companies that build concession trailers. Some are assembly line operations; others build individual trailers specifically to order. In either case, with a manufactured trailer you should be guaranteed in writing:

1. The unit is structurally sound

2. It is constructed of new material.

3. The structural components and systems are installed to code.

4. Every component is warranted.

5. Every component is documented.

A manufactured trailer is a very nice package to have. You can order a customized trailer much the same way you would order a car. For a base price you receive an aluminum box on wheels with plywood interior, and 12-volt electrical system. Options are extra; but, oh, the options! You have your choice of fold-out service windows with awnings, recessed floor, linoleum, stainless steel counters, cabinets, 120- and/or 240-volt electrical system, water system, florescent lighting, removable hitch, stabilizer jacks, marquee signs, and much more.

Manufactured concessions range from small, simple, single-axle units to the large, ornate floss wagons you see at carnivals. In fact, because many concession trailer manufacturers also manufacture utility trailers, you may have a hard time distinguishing a simple manufactured concession trailer from a concession that is a home-built conversion from a utility trailer.

Look for concession trailer manufacturers in your local directory and on the Internet. Collect catalogs and compare. Shop for specific designs and options that are important to you, as well as quality, value, service, warranty, and delivery schedule. Once you have selected a manufacturer, but before you order your trailer, use a copy of the trailer floor plan to sketch in your equipment, counters, sinks, water tanks, and storage space. Take your time and have fun. It is much easier to correct mistakes or make other changes in your plans when done in pencil than it will be later when done in stainless steel. By making several sketches of the interior design of your intended trailer, you will develop a clear vision of what your trailer, equipment, and operational needs are. You will be able to decide which interior systems you are skilled and willing enough to install yourself and which you will want to purchase as an option.

A manufactured trailer that would do well at any event, from a small festival to the carnival midway. Notice the large wrap-around windows, the inset marquee signs on the roof, and the valanced awning with signs over the large windows. The entire booth has visual depth and balance. The counters are low enough for customers to order easily.

Once you have ordered your trailer, the manufacturer will construct it with the options you have selected. After delivery, you can install the equipment you need yourself, or the manufacturer can install the equipment for you. If you plan to spend the time shopping for equipment while you are waiting for your trailer to be built, be sure to have full spec sheets of every detail of your trailer. As you shop for equipment, you will need to know the exact dimensions of each piece of required equipment as well as the exact dimensions of the allotted space into which it will be squeezed. In designing the layout of the interior, you will be trying to squeeze utility out of every possible inch of space.

Many vendors are of the opinion that manufactured trailers have a generic appearance, lacking in character. This is true of any booth that is lacking in distinctive signs, attractive menu boards, and colorful skirting. With imagination, any booth can be decorated to reflect your personality and inform the public that you are serious about what you do. The apparent quality of craftsmanship in these trailers implies to the public that your product and service are of equal quality.

New manufactured concession trailers are not cheap. Most concessionaires opt to get a few years of experience and develop a solid

Another manufactured "floss wagon" at a carnival.

lineup of events before they are willing to make this large of an investment in their concession booths.

A manufactured trailer with vinyl banner signs. This design, with wraparound windows, is very popular for a medium priced trailer.

Custom-Built Concession Trailers

After a few seasons in the business, you may come to the same conclusion about concession trailers that many vendors do. That is, if you custom design and build your trailer, you can have it exactly the way you want it. As fantastic as well-designed manufactured trailers are, they are limited by the designs and options available from the manufacturer whereas if you design and build your trailer yourself, the features and character of your trailer will only be limited by your imagination.

A booth that is custom designed is an attempt to have the best of all worlds. Being a trailer, it has the convenience and security benefits of a trailer, but it might also have other benefits that you would normally only get in a tent or pushcart. Some of the custom features I have seen include:

- Large sliding panels on three sides that, when opened, provide the openness and accessibility of a tent.

- Mounted rollout grills that slide in for travel and security and roll out when the owner is open for business. A rolled-out grill is out of the trailer, out of the way, and out where the public can see what's cooking.

- Step down removable flooring which, when removed, allows the server to stand in a pit or on the ground at eye level with the public.

- A beverage bar mounted in the wall facing the public. The customer can pour his or her own pop after purchasing a cup with ice. This enables the server to move quickly on to the next customer.

- Built in condiment pumps.

- Removable tongue that saves on the cost of space fees.

- Built-in storage compartments for hoses, electrical cords, tools, extra supplies, a generator, signs, propane bottles, pop tanks, etc.

Designing your own trailer can be a lot of fun as well as economical. But it does require a large dose of skill and knowledge to build a concession that looks good and isn't beleaguered with system failures. With a complete and accurate set of plans, a skilled craftsman can be hired to do as much or as little of the construction as you want. Many people hire a welder to build the frame, axles, and box with skin, leaving the finishing work of installing the linoleum, plumbing system, electrical system, counters, shelving, and installation of the equipment for themselves.

A custom-built concession trailer with sliding side windows and roll-out grill. The signs are hand painted on corrugated plastic and mounted in steel frames. When closed, the awning folds down, the fajita sign at the bottom folds up, and the two side windows slide forward to lock. The tongue is on the other end of the trailer.

A custom-built trailer with plenty of signs.

A custom-built trailer not quite ready to open, with sidewalls partially drawn. The banner signs are hung on removable steel pipe frames painted white. The condiment bar is built into the wrap-around stainless service counter. Barely visible at the left corner of the booth is the self-serve pop dispenser. Not visible in the picture is the drop-down floor that enables the server to stand at eye level with the customer. This concession serves on the rear of the trailer.

A custom trailer built and operated by the same concessionaire who owns the booth in the previous photo. The small booth is operated at small events, the larger booth at large events; often, both are in operation simultaneously.

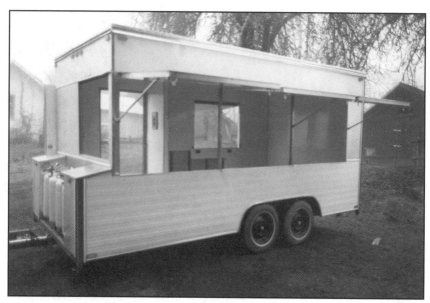

A custom trailer in the process of being built.

The same custom trailer complete and opened for business.

A custom-built BBQ trailer.

Conversion Concessions

Old RV trailers are cheap. You can get one for a song, cut in a service window, add a few sinks, install a little equipment, and be off to the races, or rather, events with a new concession business. I know it sounds too simple and a little cheesy, but this is the way a lot of concessionaires get started. And, in fact, there are many very nice conversion booths that had a previous life as something other than a concession. If you are curious enough about the business to spend a little money but are hesitant to invest a lot, using an old RV trailer or other vehicle is a good way to dabble at a few events. You can get some experience and see how you like it before putting up a larger sum of cash on a higher-quality booth and equipment.

A more moderate approach might be to purchase a used utility trailer for conversion. They are reasonably priced and, being an open slate, much easier to convert than an old RV trailer. A utility trailer has the added advantage of being built low to the ground, making it easier to cut in a service window with the right dimensions and height. Additionally, some utility trailers have a gross weight capacity capable of safely hauling the total weight of the equipment and supplies needed in your concession.

Before you get out the blowtorch and tools, become acquainted with health department regulations to be certain the unit you plan to convert can be converted. Also, be aware that RV trailers have low ceilings and high floors. Finally, don't forget to make very certain that the unit you select to convert is still roadworthy. Many old, long unused trailers have rotten tires and are cancerous with rust. Be sure to check that everything can be made into good working order and is able to haul you and your business safely down the highway.

An RV conversion. Notice the valanced awnings and hand-painted signs.

An RV conversion trailer. The custom-made sign was provided by Pepsi.

An RV conversion trailer.

A utility trailer with fold-out rear doors converted into a concession. Vinyl banner signs are mounted directly to the trailer. The menu board was provided by Coca Cola.

Pre-owned Concessions Trailers

Most new concessionaires purchase a pre-owned concession trailer, for good reason. Without prior experience in the business, they are more comfortable with a turnkey operation. They may also hope the previous owner will help out for a few events to get them started on the right foot. Without a little guidance, it is very difficult to set off down the highway into unfamiliar territory with a large, unfamiliar pile of equipment.

Finding a pre-owned concession should not be difficult for anyone with access to the Internet and who is willing to travel outside his or her neighborhood to shop. Shop locally first, then broaden your search with the use of a computer. A good plan of action may be to watch for concession trailers listed under business opportunities in the classified section of the newspaper. Try your local paper, of course, as well as newspapers from cities as far away as you are willing to drive. The local library and the Internet are good places to read newspapers not delivered to your doorstep.

When searching for a trailer on the Internet, search keywords "concession trailer." You will find dozens of sites about concession trailer manufacturing and concession classified ads. You may also want to look at an Internet message board or chat room like "google.com" or "ezboard.com." Many folks leave postings about the concession trailer they have parked in their driveway and would like to sell. The Internet auction eBay always has dozens of trailers for sale. It is a very good place to research the possibilities. Most concessions purchased on eBay are bought sight unseen. However, it may be possible to find one advertised that is located near enough to examine first-hand. If not, talk to the seller about establishing an approval contingency into the sales agreement. The important thing about buying anything from a private party over the Internet is communication. Spend as much time as you need emailing the seller with your questions. The seller should be able to send you photos of the interior and exterior of the food booth along with photos of any equipment that is included in the sale. If what you learn sounds promising, make a trip to see the booth with your own eyes before you commit to buying it.

The most common way of finding a used trailer, however, is through word of mouth. If you talk to local vendors at a nearby event, chances are one of them will know someone who has a concession trailer for sale.

The price of a used concession trailer can range anywhere from one hundred dollars to fifty thousand dollars. The price doesn't necessarily correlate to value. Compare as many trailers as you can before you buy. A preliminary phone call will answer many important questions. You may want to know when, where, and how often it was used, as well as what its gross sales were. Ask where the owner acquired it and if it is custom-built, an RV conversion, or manufactured. Ask for the dimensions, age, condition, what equipment is included, number of sinks, water storage capacity, electrical system, gross vehicle weight, number of axles, length of hitch, health department licensing status and capabilities, DMV license status, price, and terms.

By knowing in advance your menu, equipment, targeted sales volume, and licensing requirements before you shop for a trailer, you will have an idea whether the trailer and its equipment will suit your needs. Most people soon come to realize that no pre-owned and equipped trailer is perfect for them, but if they find one that has enough of the qualities and features they are looking for, they are usually willing to trade out certain pieces of equipment and make other alterations to make it just right for their purposes.

It is not uncommon for a trailer to be offered for sale along with event contracts and training for an inflated price. Be aware that with the exception of some large events, such as state and regional fairs, nearly all event contracts are offered on a year-by-year basis and are non-transferable. Who is or is not offered a contract is entirely dictated by the event coordinator. However, providing the menu remains the same, most events do offer vendors from previous years an opportunity for a new contract the following year. Depending on the quality of a seller's relationship with their event coordinators, a seller may be able to get the trailer booked into its usual events as under new management. In this case, a sales contract stipulating the contingency that a portion of the sales price is paid upon confirmation of each promised event contract would protect you from not receiving the contracts you were promised with the purchase of the trailer.

Ask to see the books. You definitely should require a look at the books if the trailer has a history of working some events, is proclaimed "a real money-maker," or, most importantly, is being purchased with event contracts. You should see for yourself firsthand what the income and expenses were for that particular booth and menu. More importantly, the gross sales will give you a good idea what volume of sales the trailer and pro-offered events are capable of. It is not uncommon for a seller to be reluctant to show the books, particularly if he or she is not retiring from the business. Many vendors guard information about their events and the money they make. Others may be very inconsistent in their bookkeeping practices.

In nearly all cases, the buyer is buying the booth, not the business. With that said, it is also important to realize that the booth you purchase must meet your expectations; otherwise, your ability to earn a financial reward will be greatly compromised. To protect yourself from arriving at your first event only to learn that nothing seems to meet the level of quality that the seller had described, ask for detailed information about any major equipment that is included, as well as the water and electrical system. The age, specifics of installation, and maintenance history will all greatly influence value. Insist that the seller show you how to operate and maintain every piece of equipment and component of the booth. The seller should be willing to walk you through a complete set-up. It would not be unreasonable to offer, along with a good-faith deposit, a letter of intent to purchase the trailer. Much like in a real estate transaction, a letter of intent would outline the agreed-upon price, terms, and the contingency that the seller provides you with a signed disclosure statement outlining his or her knowledge of the condition of every component of the proposed purchase. An additional contingency should state that the balance of the purchase price will be paid upon your final full inspection and approval. The letter of intent and the disclosure statement may or may not be legally binding. The real purpose is to promote forthrightness. If the trailer is being sold locally, many sellers will offer to go with you to your first event for training. This is the perfect time to verify that the trailer is everything it is proclaimed to be and then to pay the balance owed.

Concession Tents

A concession tent is the booth of choice for any operation that requires a lot of room for equipment, workers, preparation, and supplies. A tent is ground level, visibly open and accessible, has enough room for workers to maneuver, and is appealing to the public. In a tent, the equipment, service counter, prep area, supply storage, washing facilities, and other components can be arranged and rearranged to suit the set-up needs of an evolving operation. Vendors who sell different menus at different events have varying needs regarding equipment, workspace, and numbers of workers. Tents provide the flexibility to configure the set-up to suit their needs precisely. One of the best and possibly most important advantages is that, when viewed from the midway, concession tents are three-dimensional, lending themselves to unlimited signage and display opportunities.

Concession tents do, however, have some drawbacks. Running a concession tent is not for the physically frail. It takes a lot of muscle and endurance to unload, set up, and reload the tent, equipment, and supplies—none of which is light.

Concession tents are much more exposed to the elements than are trailers. In areas with constant wind, gas grills and fryers won't operate correctly, paper products will be blown onto the ground, and dust will get into everything. Although sidewalls can be erected to shield the contents of the booth on three sides, invariably the rain, wind, or hot afternoon sun will come from the direction of your front counter. Pole tents can be purchased with small front awnings. They are very attractive and help to keep the rain out. Because they are more open, a tent operator also has more trouble keeping out bugs, stray kids, stray dogs, and curious onlookers. In fact, it's for these reasons that some health departments require tent operators to install bug screens.

Tents are also impossible to secure from a determined thief or vandal. Some thieves will brazenly grab whatever they can reach while your back is turned. Others wait until after business hours to trespass. Many vendors put up sidewalls on all four sides when they close shop at night. Others cover the tables and contents with vinyl tarps secured with clamps. The theory is that a thief will not be so easily tempted by what he or she cannot see. On the other hand, the sidewalls provide excellent cover for the thief. Securing your business with tarps or sidewalls will also help protect it if the weather turns bad during the night.

Concession tents don't have built-in amenities such as plumbed sinks and electrical systems. Both of these systems must be installed in a temporary fashion in order to satisfy your operational needs, as well as to comply with health department regulations. Curiously, health and electrical inspectors don't look as critically at these systems in a tent as they do in a trailer. In order to provide electricity to various pieces of equipment, most vendors rely on a series of power strips and outdoor electrical cords. From the power source provided by the event, a 10–12 gauge cord supplies juice to the booth. From there, a series of cords can be either laid on the ground around the edges of the tent or secured to the frame with bungees or zip ties.

A hand-washing set-up on the outside wall of a trailer. Notice the spigoted gravity feed water, sanitary cloth bucket for wiping counters, bleach, paper towels, and a waste catch bucket on the ground.

The health inspector requires every food booth to have a three-compartment utensil washing set-up, plus a hand washing station with warm flowing water. Many tent operators set a table behind the booth where they line up three plastic dishpans for dish washing: one for washing, one for rinsing, the third for sanitizing. Also, a five-gallon (preferably insulated) spigoted water or beverage jug is set on the edge of the table where warm water can flow over your hands and into a gray water catch bucket. This is emptied into an approved receptacle (toilet) as needed or at the end of the day. An electric water kettle will quickly heat water for the hand-washing jug. With conveniently placed dish soap, bleach, hand soap, paper towels, and garbage can, the ensemble is complete.

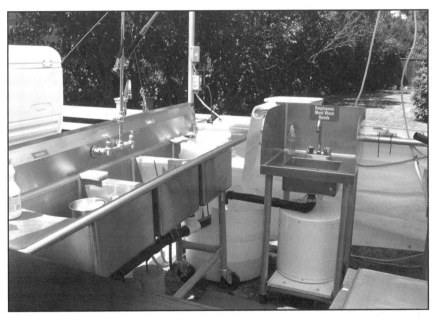

This stainless washing system is built into a tent. It is a beautiful washing set-up but likely takes many hours to assemble.

Although this washing set-up satisfies the health inspector, using small buckets of cold water is an ineffective way of cleaning a kitchen. Many tent operators have solved the problem by building their own portable, hot water plumbed sink. A frame is built using 13-square steel tubing to support a plastic laundry tub or three-compartment sink. A small 2½-gallon electric water heater is mounted on the frame, under the sink. This portable system is plumbed to receive a water hose that feeds water into the water tank, while also providing the pressure that pushes the water up through the faucet and into the sink. The gray water is drained into a five-gallon catch bucket that is emptied as needed into an approved receptacle. A lightweight plastic, three-compartment sink can be purchased (or ordered) from a restaurant equipment dealer.

A plumbed sink with hot water, paper towels, hand soap, gray water catch bucket, and a coiled auxiliary hose that extends the water supply to areas beyond the sink.

Many tent operators like to have a mat for flooring in the tent rather than having to stand on bare ground. In fact, some health departments require that the floor be covered to control dirt and dust. A 10' x 10' acrylic mat can be purchased from an RV supply store.

Some concession tents are flammable. In areas with strict fire codes, large events may require that tents be either composed of flame-resistant material or treated with an approved fire retardant. This is only a concern for vendors who attend large, highly bureaucratic events.

Instant Pop-up Canopies

An instant pop-up canopy is a pre-assembled tent constructed of lightweight aluminum tube framing and covered with a fire retardant, waterproof tarp. The frame and cover are designed to expand "accordion" style to their full dimensions. In reverse, it is easily collapsed into a compact bundle for transport and storage. A 10′ x 10′ "instant pop-up canopy is a good and economical booth to start with. It can be easily set up by one person in minutes, accommodates one to four people, and provides enough room for high-volume sales of any moderately sized menu.

As your business evolves and grows, a second 10′ x 10′ tent can be easily set up for a combined booth size of 10′ x 20′. Accessories, such as sidewalls and skirting, can also be purchased, but are fairly expensive. It may be more economical to use 10′ x 10′ plastic tarps available at any hardware store for your sidewalls. They are easily attached with small bungees. The skirting that is available is anywhere from 38" to 48" tall, higher than the standard 32" height of a folding legged table. If you don't want the skirt to hang from higher than your tables, you might be better off sewing your own skirts or hiring a local awning company to do the sewing for you. Skirts can be hung from aluminum conduit pipe or aluminum square tube. Instant pop-up canopies are available from several manufacturers. Compare prices and features online. In the spring, Costco has been known to carry a good-quality "caravan" canopy for a reasonable price. When shopping, watch for the models that have a tall, square configuration, such as EZ up "enterprise," rather than the short, angle-legged, backyard barbecue variety.

An angle-legged pop-up tent with a banner sign.

A straight legged pop-up tent with side walls up for wind protection.
The tent is tied down to water fill plastic barrels on each corner.

Pole Tents

Pole tents are commonly seen on the midway at carnivals. They have all of the attractions of a pop-up, plus they are sturdier, last longer, and look much more professional. However, they are also heavier, requiring more people and time to set up and tear down. They need more room to store. And, of course, they cost more.

Most pole tents are framed with 2″ to 3″ steel or aluminum poles that assemble like tinker toys and are covered with heavy laminate vinyl. They can be ordered in a variety of colors or combination of colors and have a variety of accessories available, such as sidewalls, awnings, and skirts. Sometimes used tents are available from local shops that rent tents and equipment to special events and weddings. In recent years, Costco has been known to carry an economical 10′ x 15′ shelter kit package of 2″ plastic frame poles, which are covered with lightweight plastic tarp. It is similar in design to a pole tent but with less weight, quality, and cost. Other vendors build their own pole tents. They may purchase the poles from a pole dealer, then purchase heavy tarps from a hardware store for the roof and sides.

A 20′ pole tent. The banner signs are hung on steel poles with bungee.

Whether you use a pop-up or a pole tent, it is important to fasten it securely to the ground in the event of a windstorm. Both can be secured with stakes into the ground or by lashing them down to tables that are weighted with heavy equipment or barrels of water. No one wants his or her equipment destroyed by a blowing tent. More importantly, a tumbling tent is extremely dangerous to anyone in its path.

An economy plastic pole tent. The banner sign is hanging as a skirt from the service counter.

A tent entirely made with steel frame covered with plastic tarp.

A pole tent with vinyl skirting and tarp roof.

Stick Joints

Stick joints, sometimes affectionately referred to as "throw-ups," are temporarily constructed rigid booths usually built of wood but can be made of almost anything. They have advantages similar to pole tents, such as visibility, accessibility, maneuverability, and sturdiness, and are also economical. They also have many of the same disadvantages, such as being exposed to the elements and also being physically difficult to set up. The beauty of stick joints is that the wall panels (usually interlocking panels) can be elaborately painted and provide a great place for advertising your menu. The counters can be designed as an integral part of the booth construction, eliminating the need to hang skirts or using folding tables. Many stick joints take advantage of their ability to provide service counters on three or four sides, which greatly increases their sales exposure. No two stick joints are the same. They can range from a simple wooden box to a booth that is radiating character.

This stick joint is owned by a couple from Australia. They spend the summer in the States selling food and the winter in Australia running a dive shop. What a life!

A stick joint next to a manufactured trailer. Notice how the stick joint's sidewalls are an integral part of the booth, creating good weather protection while not hindering sales.

A nonprofit stick joint with hand-painted signs.

A small nonprofit stick joint, a large stick joint, and a pop-up tent.

Motorized Vans

Concession vans are popular in many communities as rolling roadside restaurants. They are less frequently seen on the midway at fairs and festivals. At these types of venues they have similar advantages and disadvantages as concession trailers. Licensing requirements are the same as any other temporary concession. One reason they are less popular than other types of concessions is because, though they may be perfect for making quick sales at stops in industrial parks, they are not designed to compete, visually, on a midway. Additionally, acquiring insurance may be a little more difficult. Vehicle insurers classify them as business vehicles. Business liability insurers see higher risk in the form of a combustible engine.

A custom-built concession van with a built-in pop dispenser. The awning is rolled out.

A van conversion with the awning rolled up.

Pushcarts

No one can deny the charming appeal of pushcarts, commonly seen on street corners and in parks of nearly every large city. Pushcarts seem to embody the independent, simple, yet moderately prosperous lifestyle many of us crave. For anyone who wants to earn money with a small and simple operation, a pushcart may be the best type of booth.

In the Northwest, pushcarts are often seen selling espresso. This is due in part to the popularity of espresso coffee in this part of the country. Reasonably-priced espresso carts are frequently advertised in the classifieds. Many of these carts are fairly new and fully equipped with all the required espresso equipment as well as a hand washing sink and small refrigerator. From a food handling logistical perspective, espresso is fairly simple. The only ingredients on the menu that need refrigeration are milk and whipped cream. Utensil cleaning is not difficult because there is no cooking or grease involved. Ice cream is another dish that lends itself well to pushcarts, as are hot dogs. A steam pan for dogs, another for buns, a few condiments, and you're in business. However, due to their small size, whatever you sell from a pushcart must need only a minimal amount of equipment.

A homemade pushcart.

The health department requires that pushcart operators comply with the same regulations as any temporary restaurant booth; therefore, you will need to have a utensil and hand-washing set-up on a table behind your pushcart.

Pushcarts do have a few drawbacks. They are very exposed to the elements. Many pushcart operators set up under a pop-up tent. The tent offers protection from the weather as well as some security at night. Their sales capacity is limited by their size. Also, they are small and easily overlooked by potential customers, particularly when they are set up among larger and more prominent food booths.

Here's a tip: Pushcart operators frequently must purchase a full 10' x 10' booth space, the minimum size. It makes sense to make use of the entire space by setting up a pop-up tent or side tables for the extra sales capacity and sales exposure.

Look for pushcarts in the classifieds and on the web. Another viable option for acquiring a pushcart is to build one yourself. Large wheeled carts are easier to maneuver than ones with small wheels. Wheels, axle, plywood, and hardware can be purchased from your local hardware store. An attractive six-foot patio umbrella provides some protection from the elements and creates vital visual appeal.

Most people use a utility trailer with a ramp to transport their pushcarts. Because the supply needs are relatively minor, a trailer should easily hold your cart, related equipment, and all of your supplies.

Size Matters—Is Bigger Better?

After considering all of the different types of booths, along with the advantages and disadvantages of each type, some thought should be given to the size of your booth. The size of your booth will have both a positive and a negative impact on many aspects of your business.

Operating costs. A large booth is more expensive to buy, equip, and operate than a small booth. Space fees at many events are determined by midway frontage. A large booth may need to be towed by a larger and more expensive vehicle. And a large booth may require more workers to operate effectively.

Logistical considerations. A small booth is easier to manage whereas a large booth requires more time and effort to transport, set up, maintain, and operate.

Sales capacity. A large booth can accommodate more equipment, inventory, product, and workers, all of which increase sales capacity and influence a booth's ability to achieve critical mass. The size of a booth's menu and its ability to achieve a high volume of sales is, in almost all cases, dictated by the size of the booth. A large booth will also accommodate enough workers to keep the operation flowing smoothly and efficiently.

Sales appeal. Equally important is the frequently overlooked fact that, for several reasons, a large booth has the potential to attract more business. A large booth has the capacity to handle not only a larger menu but also a higher volume of product available for sale. This, in turn, implies professionalism and promotes business. The public's perception is that professional booths provide faster service and better food. Also, a small booth can become concealed and appear stifled by its line of customers whereas, with a large booth, the line of customers not only doesn't conceal the booth but instead creates an aura of status. Finally, because it takes longer to stroll past a large booth, it has a larger window of opportunity to influence people to stop and buy.

Booking opportunities. A small booth has the advantage of being much easier to book into events. Many events have a limited number of spaces available for food booths. A twenty-foot booth requires two 10′ spaces whereas a 10′ booth requires only one. Also, in some cases, coordinators will shoehorn a small pushcart into a space where no other booth would fit. The advantage of greater booking opportunities is even more apparent when it comes to selecting events. A lean and mean small booth can easily swoop in and out of one-day events.

A booth that is self-contained and can be set up in one hour can take advantage of vacant fields, street corner parades, and ballpark events that a large booth could not even consider. Many vendors own two booths. They use a large, high-sales capacity booth at big five-day fairs and a small pushcart or trailer at one-day festivals and auctions. A vendor with the manpower to run both booths simultaneously all season is a vendor who makes money.

In general, a large booth will outsell a small booth, but there's no guarantee. If other marketing principles are not applied and if any of the many other factors that influence sales are not in place (see Chapter 13), a large booth will not be an asset but will only cause you to suffer from its disadvantages.

Here's a tip: If you plan to do only one or two events or want to get your feet wet in the business without investing in a booth or vehicles, many event grounds, such as city parks and county fairgrounds, have booths in permanent structures that can be rented by vendors and nonprofits. Little concession trailers can also be rented from Pepsi Cola.

A Pepsi Cola concession trailer available for rent. This one is selling T-shirts.

A small structure for rent at a fair.

A double structure for rent at a fair.

A manufactured trailer with banner signs mounted on the roof and marquee signs mounted to the awnings. On the back side of the trailer is a pop-up tent used for extra storage and prep.

The trailer on the left is an RV conversion. The trailer on the right is custom-built. The service window on both trailers opens on the rear. Both trailers have hand-painted signs.

A custom-built concession trailer, tongue, and rear view. Notice the generator and electrical cords stored inside the large storage compartment (door open) on the tongue. The entry door on the back of the trailer is open.

CHAPTER 6

Choosing, Buying, or Building Your Food Service Equipment

Food service equipment falls into three categories: major equipment, such as deep fryers and grills; minor equipment, such as hot dog steamers and heat lamps; and small wares, such as ice chests, tongs, and ice scoops. It makes sense that your food service equipment ensemble will be dictated by the menu that you plan to serve. Perhaps you see yourself running a one-man operation selling a single dish. In this case, your equipment needs will be minimal. On the other hand, if you plan to operate a high-volume, multi-dish menu, your equipment will be more elaborate. In either case, the equipment you use should be capable of meeting the demands of your operation. In most cases, the main dish on the menu and the equipment required to prepare that dish will be the focal point of the operation.

Selecting Your Major and Minor Equipment

One of the best ways to learn about food service equipment, get some menu ideas, and do some brainstorming, is to visit a new and used restaurant equipment dealer. You will be amazed by what you see. There is a piece of food service equipment designed to do every conceivable task involving food service. You will also notice that most pieces of major equipment are made of stainless steel, built to withstand heavy use, and cost a bundle compared to a similar piece of equipment designed for use in your home. With food preparation equipment, it is important to understand the difference in function and capabilities between that made for commercial use and that for domestic use. For reasons of food safety, the health department may require certain equipment, such as refrigerators and freezers, to be stickered as approved by the NSF (National Sanitation Foundation). As you can imagine, a domestic freezer is not capable of keeping ice cream bars hard when you open the door to pull one out five hundred times a day. Nor is a domestic refrigerator used in commercial food service able to maintain the required 45-degree (or lower) temperature needed to prevent bacterial growth. And, although not required to be stickered by the NSF, a "fry daddy" is simply not capable of deep-frying one hundred corn dogs an hour. But then, on the other hand, who needs a commercial microwave when its only job is occasionally to thaw frozen hot dog buns?

Certain types of equipment lend themselves more readily to menu variation than others. For instance, a griddle or grill can be used for cooking hamburgers, hot dogs, bratwurst, eggs, pancakes, fajitas, quesadillas, and much more whereas an espresso machine or soft-serve ice cream freezer is not capable of doing anything other than what it was designed for. If you want to be able to expand or vary your menu without purchasing ever more equipment, consider carefully your equipment's capabilities and limitations.

All major food service equipment runs on power, either electrical or gas. It is very important that you restrict your electrical consumption needs to a minimum by using propane (LP) powered equipment whenever possible. Most events have a limited amount of electricity available for vendors, and power outages are common. Many event applications ask for a list of your electric appliances. If your amperage needs are too high, you will not be offered a contract. Also, be wary of equipment that uses 220V of electricity. Very few events can provide you with a large enough outlet. In fact, power outages are so common that many concessionaires carry a small generator for backup. By using liquid propane powered equipment whenever possible, you will be more likely to keep operating during an electrical failure. Equipment that runs on natural gas can be converted for liquid propane by the equipment dealer.

When you get ready to shop for major equipment, collect catalogs from an assortment of dealers, both restaurant supply stores and manufacturers. Even if you plan to purchase used equipment, the catalogs will provide the specs of the various models. With that information, you can compare the prices of apples to apples from one dealer to the next and also target your search for the model with correct dimensions and capacity when talking with private parties or auctions.

Prices can vary from shop to shop. When negotiating with a dealer, you might get a much better deal if you are equipped with a lower priced competitors catalog. This is particularly true if you are buying several pieces. You can save about fifty percent by buying used, reconditioned equipment rather than new. The value of new equipment depreciates the minute it leaves the store. A reputable used equipment dealer will offer a warranty. Large and/or elaborate pieces should be delivered and installed by the dealer.

You might find an even better deal if you watch the papers for restaurant liquidations and auctions. Most new restaurants go out of business. Many are faced with consigning their shiny new equipment back to the supplier where they will be lucky to recoup twenty percent of its value. Many restaurant owners who are in this situation are happy to get any price above twenty percent that they can. There are several drawbacks to buying used equipment from a private party. First, there are no warranties. Second, you must haul and install it yourself. Third, it may be hard to find the piece with the precise dimensions and capacity that you need. Fourth, unless you are familiar with the type of equipment you are shopping for, you would be unlikely to recognize a good buy or a bad one. Fifth and most importantly, used equipment has a higher probability of breaking down. The last thing you want is your equipment to fail during a busy event.

Building Your Own Equipment

One of the great advantages of running a food concession business as opposed to running a restaurant is that you can build much of your equipment yourself. It would be ridiculous to spend thousands of dollars on heavy stainless cabinets whose main purpose is to provide a source of heat for steam pans when a custom-built piece will serve the same purpose, better fit it into its allotted space, and, pay a fraction of the price. Many concession menus are cooked on a grill, in a wok, or in a pot of boiling water. They are then held hot and served from a steam pan. You can build all of these devices yourself and easily save several thousand dollars. With propane burners (available at any propane equipment and supply store), welded steel, copper tubing, and a little ingenuity, you can design and build your own equipment that will do the job of heating steel plates for grilling or steaming water in your hot-holding steam pans. Not only will you save yourself a lot of money, but you can also customize your equipment for size and weight. However, be very careful in your design that you allow for insulation or airspace between the burners and your walls or countertop. If you plan to go this route, visit a large used restaurant equipment supply store where you can pick up used steam pans, pan inserts, and pan racks. You may find shelves upon shelves of miscellaneous items that can be used on your project.

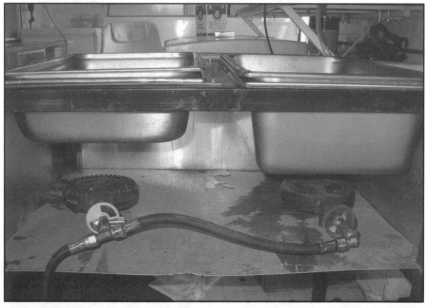

Homemade steam pans. Over two propane burners is a welded steel frame holding two double pans. The lower pans hold water for steam. The pan inserts hold the food.

If you are using a concession trailer, exhaust from propane as well as greasy cooking fumes should be vented to the outside with a ventilation hood. Be aware that some state fire marshals additionally require that exhaust hoods have a built-in fire suppression system. Restaurant exhaust systems are expensive. The cost may detour your plans to custom build your own concession trailer. In states where the authorities are not so particular, you might get by with using sheet metal to line a trap door or electric vent fan built into the roof or high on the wall above the cooking area. In either case, for cleaning purposes the wall behind any equipment that cooks with grease should be lined with narrow gauge sheet metal or stainless steel. The presence of greasy fumes and propane exhaust in a concession tent are not usually a serious consideration with the fire marshal. If they are a concern, some fire marshals will allow a vendor to use a plywood cover to smother the fire instead of requiring the installation of a fire suppression hood.

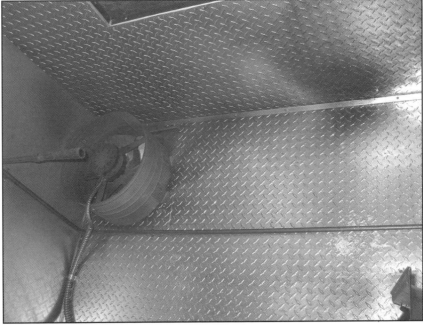

A homemade hood/vent/fire suppression over a deep fryer in a trailer. The tube in front of the fan is attached to a fire extinguisher mounted outside the hood. It is triggered by hand in the event of a fire.

Three deep fryers. Two have homemade chimneys to divert the exhaust outside the tent.

Any product that is displayed or prepared within reach of the germy public is required to be protected with a sneeze guard. Most vendors build something that will suit their purpose out of lightweight ¼-"clear acrylic. More expensive polycarbonate can be bent and formed without breaking and makes an attractive guard. Hot displays of food should be protected with shatterproof glass rather than acrylic. Equipment outside the confines of your booth should also be protected with a railing of some sort, particularly if it is hot or creates any risk to the public. Almost any problem can be solved and almost any need filled by custom designing and building (or having built) the perfect piece of equipment or hardware to serve your purpose. You can easily get ideas from other vendors. This is one subject on which they are not so reticent and may even welcome the opportunity to display their ingenuity.

Glass sneeze guards protecting hot food under heat lamps on the front counter.

A homemade corn roaster next to a pop-up tent.

A pole tent with banner sign. Partial sidewalls are installed for weather protection. The grill on the side is fenced to protect the public.

A homemade BBQ.

Propane Power

With equipment that runs on propane, you will need to purchase propane tanks and a regulator. Most vendors use propane tanks ranging in size from ten to thirty gallons. The total volume you need will depend on the BTU (British thermal unit) capacity of your equipment. Some vendors haul several ten-gallon tanks because they are easy to handle while others prefer the expanded mileage they get from a large thirty-gallon tank. The propane leaves the tank at high pressure and must be regulated down to low pressure with a regulator before it reaches your equipment. It is safer to mount the regulator on the tank

This ten-gallon propane tank is connected to equipment from the rear of the trailer.

so that the line to the equipment will not be pressurized and prone to leak. However, if the line from the tank to the equipment is long, you might consider regulating at the equipment. That way, the propane delivered through the line to the equipment at high pressure ensures the equipment will always receive enough juice to operate effectively.

Propane tanks are heavy and can be knocked over easily. Whether you have your propane tanks mounted on the tongue of your trailer, setting behind your trailer or tent, or transport them in the back of a truck, they must always be securely fastened. In fact, the fire marshal may have a look to see that that is the case.

Small Wares

No matter your menu, your equipment list for small wares will be amazingly long. These are the tools of your trade, and there is a required tool for every aspect of your food service business. Spend time in your imagination with a pen and paper while you visualize yourself walking through every activity. List everything needed in your entire process of buying your supplies, transporting, storing, pre-prep, post-prep, cooking, displaying, hot holding, cold holding, and serving

Here's a tip. Only a few concessionaires use refrigerators. Most operations use such a large quantity of product that a refrigerator is useless and only adds weight and takes up space. Most vendors use ice chests instead. Whether they are thawing cases of frozen product or storing cases or tubs of various ingredients, they can utilize ice chests much more efficiently. By carefully monitoring the ice at the bottom, creating a barrier between melting ice and the product, and laying several heavy paper grocery bags under the lid for added insulation, the product keeps as cold as in a refrigerator. Use a separate chest for each product to avoid cross contaminations and monitor the temperature with a thermometer inside each chest. A tidy stack of ice chests under a tarp behind a booth will make for a booth that means business.

each component of your menu. Don't forget the condiments and paper products. You will arrive at a list of containers, tools, and equipment that is frightening. The conundrum is that you need these tools to do your first event, but you won't get a real understanding of what you actually do and do not need until you have done the event. Many small items, such as plastic containers and trash cans, are priced lower at house ware stores than at restaurant supply stores and will see you through just fine until you've done a few events.

Designing Your Signs

There are as many different kinds of signs on food booths as there are food booths. Signs do more than advertise. They communicate business identity and level of professionalism. They also distinguish one booth from the next. Therefore, a lot of thought should go into the design and production of your sign.

Look at the signs on the various food booths at an event. Notice how well they catch your eye and advertise their product. Also, notice the material they are made of and how they are mounted to the booth. There are hundreds of ways to make a sign and to attach it to a booth, from crayon on poster board with duct tape, to flashing, backlit marquees. A good middle-of-the-road and economical option is to visit your local sign shop. For a reasonable price, you can have made a sign in many colors on any of many materials, including vinyl banner or corrugated plastic. A small graphics program on your computer is very helpful in designing a sign with character. Giving a copy of your design to the sign shop will help you to have your sign built exactly the way you want it. Shop around for the best price.

Some people like to save money by making their own signs. Unless you have artistic talent above amateur level, I would give careful consideration to this option. The end result may be a sign that looks cheap and reflects poorly on your business. However, professionally-made signs are not cheap. Frequently, a cash-strapped vendor or one who needs a temporary sign to try a new menu idea will make one on corrugated plastic with stencils or stick-on letters. Sheets of corrugated plastic as large as 4′ x 8′ can be purchased for a reasonable price from any sign shop. The most important thing is to have an attractive sign that catches the eye from a distance.

Corporations are eager to help you sell their products. If you are selling a name brand product, such as Coca Cola or Pepsi Cola beverages, Tillamook ice cream, Starbucks Coffee, Oscar Meyer Wieners, Foster Farm corn dogs, Moore onion rings, Armour wieners, Frito-Lay tortilla chips, Garden Burger hamburgers, Jet Tea smoothies, or even Heinz ketchup, to name only a few, the companies will be happy to help boost your sales with a banner, window sticker, or sign to hang on your booth. Call up the distributor in your area to learn what they will contribute to help you sell their product. You will be amazed how much branding, i.e., associating your business with a specific name brand, can make a difference in your sales. Brand recognition establishes validity as well. If you want to boast you use only the finest ingredients, stick a logo on your booth of a brand you use that's known for its quality.

Two homemade sandwich board signs. The one on the left is framed with PVC pipe. The sign hangs loosely from chains inside the frame, so the wind won't easily knock it over.

Vinyl banners and corrugated plastic signs are commonly hung on aluminum conduit or steel pipe above a booth. Some vendors hang their signs from poles; others lash them with bungees to a frame. A vinyl banner can be rolled for easy storage. Vent holes can be cut in vinyl so it will behave in a windstorm. However, unless a banner is lashed tightly within a pipe frame, it will be prone to bulge or wrinkle. Corrugated plastic signs, being rigid, take more room to store, and act like a kite in the wind. Vinyl banners are generally less expensive than plastic signs. Refer to chapter 13, Marketing Your Product, for more information about signs.

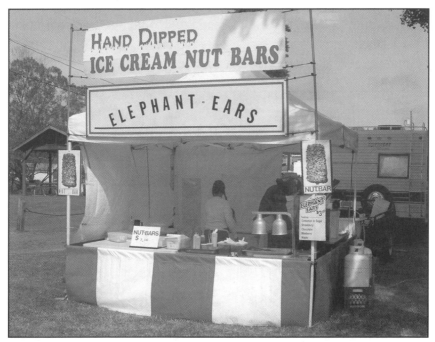

A pop-up tent with corrugated plastic signs attached by bungee to aluminum pipe. All the signs are simple, easy to read, and straight to the point. Notice the propane tanks set in milk crates on the side of the tent. The milk crates help prevent the tanks from tipping over.

Menu Boards

A menu board is a different but related component of your sign. Most vendors choose to hang a large, eye-catching sign high on their booths that advertises important items on their menus. They then use a smaller sign down low where the public can easily read the prices and details. Many vendors rely on Pepsi or Coke menu boards to display their menu and prices. These are frequently given freely to vendors who sell soda pop. The little plastic blue letters are easily changed or rearranged, making them easy to use and read. And the Pepsi or Coke logo promotes sales. Some concessions go a step further by sporting custom-designed menu boards complete with photos and a description of each item on their menus. A menu board is an important sales tool. Using only the finest or freshest ingredients in your food won't help your sales unless you tell people about them. If your barbeque sauce runs off the plate, say so. If your burgers are the biggest and juiciest, take a photo, blow it up, laminate it, and put it on your menu board. Once your big sign leads folks to stand in front of your booth, it's time to seal the deal with a good sales pitch on your menu board.

This hand-painted sign ingeniously doubles as a menu board.

Lighting for a Better Bottom Line

Many events go strong even after the sun has set. This is the time of day that the temperature becomes more comfortable, people are off work, evening entertainment is in full swing, and the joint really gets jumping. At dusk, a whole new visual sales tool is available to you as many of your unlit competitors fade into darkness. Quality of lighting is a critical element in a booth's ability to stand out from the competition and to influence sales. Lights cost very little. And yet, irrationally, many new vendors apparently prefer that their booths be obscured by near darkness to dishing out a few bucks for decent lights.

Fluorescent lights inside your booth draw attention like a lit stage in a darkened theater. Don't just light your booth's interior. Direct lights on your signs on the outside of your booth as well. Your customers need to see what you're selling. Many vendors use clamp lights

An ice cream push cart is set in front of a pop-up tent. The tent provides extra room and weather protection for freezers and stock. The booth is well lit at night, with a clamp light shining up onto the top sign.

for outside lighting. They are easily installed and easily removed for traveling. Many vendors use amber lights when moths and other night-flying insects become a problem. The health department wants interior lights to be shielded. If they break, glass can easily get into the food. Florescent tube lights can be covered with acrylic sleeves available at Cash and Carry.

Booth Interior Design

No matter which type of booth you use, when planning the interior of your booth, the first thing you need is the health department handbook of regulations. Under a temporary restaurant permit, you can take an empty shell of a trailer and install only the equipment you need for storing food, preparing food, and serving food, as long as it is done according to health department regulations. Just as with a tent, you need only a minimal system to ensure your hands and utensils are cleaned, the food is kept at the appropriate temperature, and your procedure for preparing and serving food does not spread bacteria. Although temporary concessions aren't required to have plumbed sinks or water tanks, you might want to make your life easier by permanently installing sinks with plumbing. After all, one of the benefits of using a trailer is the added convenience of hot and cold running water, water tanks, both fresh and gray, and equipment installed permanently so it doesn't need to be manhandled every time you go to an event. A (potable) garden hose can be your source of water, but if you are self-contained with fresh and gray water tanks, a larger variety of venues will be available for you to attend. An inexpensive and logical way to get into the business is to use an empty shell of a trailer or tent and only install the bare essentials for doing your job and passing the health inspection. Later, after you are more familiar with the business and have a clearer idea what you want in your booth, you can permanently install electric and water systems, cabinets and counters, and food service equipment. This is a particularly good idea if you aren't yet certain about your menu. It would be a shame to spend a lot of money and time installing a set-up for grilled food if the following season you might be selling deep fried food instead.

If you have never worked in a food service establishment, you may not appreciate the importance of work flow and work triangles. No matter what type of concession you use, it is important to arrange your equipment, service counter, and preparation area in a way that the staff can get the work done efficiently, with the fewest number of steps and without stepping on each other. If you work alone, your work triangle will be small. If you have a staff of four, your triangle will be large or you may have several triangles. You should start with a list of all the equipment you will need and all the tasks that will be performed. Then draw a floor plan of your booth. Mark in all of your equipment, work surfaces, food preparation area, food displays area, storage areas, service area, and cash register.

The back of a pop-up tent. This is the view the public doesn't often see. Ice chests, cases of product, and plastic totes everywhere. These vendors use plastic folding tables for counter surfaces. Both grills are homemade. One is mounted with its propane tanks on a wheeled cabinet. The folding chair is leaning against a hand washing sink built into a wooden box.

The interior design should be set up to accommodate the right number of workers. Divide the booth into workstations. Each worker should be able to get the job done without crossing paths with another worker. Also, each worker should take as few steps as possible.

The difference between taking one step or two steps from the pop dispenser to the cash register can add up to many miles of steps over the course of the summer.

The interior of a smoothie booth. This set-up is for a staff of two. A work station and cash register are on each side of the booth. The helper is swatting a rag at yellow jackets, which are common with a sweet menu.

CHAPTER 7

On the Road

Travel Vehicles and Equipment

Your vehicle (or combination of vehicles) is an important component of your business. Which type and how many vehicles you use will depend on what you are transporting, how many drivers you have available, and the size of your vehicle budget. The fewer drivers you have, the more you will need to select vehicles that will serve more than one purpose. Your vehicles must do a combination of some or all of the following things:

- *Transport your concession.* A trailer must be towed by a motorized vehicle. A tent, stick joint, or pushcart is likely transported inside a vehicle.

- *Haul your equipment and supplies.* If you have a trailer concession, your equipment will ride inside the concession trailer. If you use a concession tent or stick joint, your equipment will be transported inside a vehicle, probably next to your bundled-up concession. And no matter what type of concession you have, unless you have an extra vehicle and driver to run for additional supplies, you will need a stock vehicle large enough to bring all your stock with you.

- *Provide a place to live while at an event.* Most special events are too far from home to allow you to commute back and forth each day. Vendors sleep on the seat of the truck, inside a stock vehicle, on the floor of the concession (though the health department may not approve), in an RV, or in a motel room. Sleeping arrangements for your staff are also important.

- *Be a "go-pher."* Stocking up, both between events and possibly while at an event, requires a vehicle that can haul everything you need.

Vehicles are expensive to buy, maintain, license, insure, and fuel. In fact, the purchase and operation of motorized vehicles might constitute the largest expense in the concession budget. Therefore, concessionaires are extremely creative when it comes to solving the problem of how to accomplish all the previously mentioned tasks with the fewest number of vehicles. Some vendors like to travel light. They may simply use a pickup truck to transport their concessions. After setting up, they use the truck to go purchase their supplies. At night, they either sleep in the booth, on the seat of the truck, or they get a motel room. Frequently, couples who enjoy some comfort while on the road will use two vehicles. One driver may haul a fifth-wheel motor home with a pickup truck, which provides a place to live and a "go-pher" vehicle. The other driver hauls the concession trailer with a stock truck. Most vendors who spend a lot of time on the road configure their assortment of vehicles to include a motor home. However, motor homes generally cannot be adapted to serve a second purpose. Therefore, some vendors will instead modify a stock trailer or truck to include living quarters. They may not be living with all the same luxuries of a motor home, but by configuring the vehicle to serve more than one purpose, they save money. With a nice RV, what you gain in comfort you lose in

> At large events the vendor parking area might look like a vehicle freak show. You will see everything from pickup trucks, campers, motor homes, and fifth wheels, to stock trailers, box vans, step vans, buses, tractor/trailers, passenger vans, and shuttle buses, most of which have been modified with various levels of craftsmanship to suit their owners' needs.

storage capacity and power. However, if your business keeps you on the road, comfort may be more important than anything else. Many retirees live in large motor homes and use a concession business to support their lifestyles. Other concessionaires follow the event season across the country. In the heat (and tornadoes) of summer, they move north. When the weather cools in the fall, they move south. Even if you don't live on the road, it is important to have enough comfort so you don't burn out from lack of sleep or because you can't tolerate discomfort while you're away doing your job. All of us have different needs when it comes to personal comfort.

When considering your options, there are a few things you need to consider:

- If you plan to pull a concession trailer with a large motor home or truck, you might have a difficult time maneuvering the concession on the crowded grounds of an event.

- The floor of a concession trailer is a good place to haul extra supplies such as garbage cans and extra cases of product. However, the trailer floor alone is rarely able to haul enough supplies to do an event without overloading the trailer. Additionally, if you use the floor of your trailer for transporting supplies, the stock must be unloaded and put somewhere else before you can get to work.

- Some vendors prefer to sleep at an event in a motor home. They like to be near their booths during the night for security and then conveniently wake up in the morning already on-site. During the long days of a long event, a nearby RV provides a place to freshen up, grab a snack, or take a nap.

- For some vendors, a comfortable and spacious motel room with a bed, TV, and hot morning shower is an advantage over a cramped motor home.

- Some vendors use a motor home for themselves but have the hired help make their own arrangements by sleeping in a pup tent, in the supply vehicle, or on the floor of the booth.

Concession trailers and stock trailers, once loaded with equipment and stock, can easily become extremely heavy. Be sure the vehicle you choose to haul a trailer is up for the job. As mentioned in Chapter 5, Designing Your Booth, a truck larger than the standard 3/4 ton may be needed to tow a trailer that weights over 6,500 pounds. This is particularly true if the pickup is loaded with a camper or stock. Load levelers can help equalize the weight between two units and bridge the gap between being unsafe or having to invest in a larger vehicle. If you are like most vendors and have a limited amount of start-up capital, you may be inclined to use older vehicles rather than purchase newer ones. Unfortunately, older vehicles are more likely to break down. If you break down on the way to an event, you risk not only the cost of repairs but also the loss of revenue from the event. If you are pulling a trailer with the vehicle that needs to be towed, many towing companies will not tow a vehicle while it is attached to a trailer. The result is that you must either leave your trailer on the side of the highway or hire two tow trucks. If you own AAA or other travel insurance, confirm that your policy is adequate for your assortment of vehicles. I know several vendors who had insult added to injury when they learned at a time of crisis that theirs was not.

Support Vehicles

There are many ways to transport a concession booth, inventory, and equipment to an event. The components of your own concession vehicle puzzle must be configured to accommodate your particular needs. The type, size, and amount of stuff you haul, the number of available drivers you have, and the size of your budget will determine which type of stock vehicle or vehicles are right for you.

There is one particular situation many concessionaires encounter that best illustrates the logistical brainstorming that must take place when it comes to configuring your menu, booth, equipment, and support vehicles. Concessionaires often need as many as three or more freezers running at all times. Between events, the freezers are at home stocked full of product waiting to go to an event. Weekly, the freezers are transported to an event where they keep the product frozen and available for sale. After the event, the freezers and unsold stock go home again until the following event. This is a simple enough scenario, with no simple solution. Here are some ways a concessionaire might approach the problem:

- Use a concession trailer big enough to keep three freezers in at all times. However, freezers are heavy and take up a lot of space. Therefore, the trailer would need to be so large as to require a large vehicle to tow it and the purchase of extra booth space at events.

- Have enough manpower available to load and unload the freezers in and out of a vehicle for each transport. At the event, the freezers could be unloaded from the vehicle and kept running behind the booth then reloaded into a vehicle for the trip home.

- Keep the freezers in a stock vehicle. At the event, the stock vehicle should ideally be parked near the booth for access to the contents and a power outlet. If it must be parked away from the booth, a generator will be needed to keep the freezers running.

- Keep three freezers at home, one in the concession trailer and two in the garage. When leaving for an event, transfer the stock from the two freezers in the garage into ice chests. Use the freezer in the concession to rotate product out of the ice chests so nothing thaws out prematurely and spoils. This is a good and viable solution for many products. However, it is not a good solution for ice cream or ice. And it still requires the transport and handling of one large, heavy freezer.

Stock vehicles are critical to large operations. No large concession business, whether it operates with a trailer or tent, can manage without an extra vehicle for hauling and storing equipment, stock, propane bottles, water hoses, electric cords, freezers, ice chests, tools, cases of paper products, garbage cans, a ladder, and so on. The job is much easier if the stock vehicle is designed to store and haul all of these things efficiently. The business needs to be restocked at least weekly, and, during an event, the staff will dive into the stock vehicle repeatedly to grab something that is quickly needed. Time and energy

A little utility trailer parked behind a van conversion concession. The trailer has been customized with a freezer unit built into the front half of the trailer. The rear half is for non-frozen product. This is a nice package of vehicles. The concession van tows the little stock trailer.

The rear of a custom-built trailer. The awning off the back of the booth provides a sheltered area for storage and prep. The stock truck conveniently parked in back holds extra stock.

will be preserved if freezers and shelving are installed where they can be easily accessed during an event and restocked between events without unloading other items that are in the way. It is nice to know exactly where your wrenches or duct tape are stored when you have a minor emergency on your hands. The weight must also be balanced for safety.

Stock Trailers

One of the most efficient and common ways to transport equipment and stock is with a utility trailer. They come in a variety of sizes, can be wired for electricity to keep freezers running during and between events, and they can double as living quarters with the installation of a few amenities. Unlike a

Here's a tip: Although many events can provide room behind your booth for a small utility trailer, very few can provide room for a large stock truck. More events will accommodate your stock trailer behind your booth if it is not longer than your booth space is wide.

A motor home and stock trailer with a fold down ramp. These concessionaires use a stick joint, which they transport along with stock in the stock trailer. They live in the motor home and travel across the country doing events.

pickup truck or other multiuse vehicle, trailers don't need to be unloaded and loaded repeatedly for cleaning or when needed for other purposes. When purchasing a stock trailer, consider the type of doors you need. Many trailers over 12' long have a man door toward the tongue for easy entrance and a large drop-down gate on the rear that doubles as a ramp. Some trailers have double rear doors that swing out. In these cases, a portable ramp can be built from two lengths of 2" x 12" lumber. Ramparts can be purchased at hardware or RV supply stores. Trailers are low to the ground and easy to load and unload.

Stock Trucks

There is a limitless variety of large vehicles that can be used as a stock truck. Like stock trailers, they can be wired and plumbed to accommodate freezers for storage and living quarters. Heavy stock vehicles can also haul a heavy concession trailer. Many heavy trucks have a bed as high as 4' and require a lift gate for loading and unloading. The downside is that heavy trucks are considered commercial vehicles and are expensive to purchase, operate, insure, license, and maintain. In some cases, these costs can be reduced when a large truck is made into a customized motor home and licensed with the DMV as a motor home.

A large pole tent at a fair with the stock truck parked near the booth.

CHAPTER 8

How Much Will This Cost?
Budgeting for Success

Start-up Costs

Compared with starting nearly any other business with the same potential earnings, a concession can be started fairly inexpensively. The size of your budget will determine your selection of booth and equipment, choice of menu, size of operation, distance you travel, and selection of vehicles. If you plan a menu with minimal equipment requirements, already have appropriate vehicles, and intend to try out a few shows with the smallest investment possible, you can start a concession for less than five thousand dollars. Many new concessionaires wisely choose to get into the business as inexpensively as possible. They realize that without the benefit of experiencing some events, they can't possibly know enough about the business to make a large investment comfortably. They may start with a pop-up tent and some used equipment and make do with their less-than-new pickup truck. However, the problem with starting too small is that without making a large enough investment, they don't give themselves a fair opportunity to succeed. The failure rate of new vendors is extremely high. But it doesn't have to be that way. Most new vendors either can't or won't spend enough on their new enterprise either to look or feel like they mean business. As a result, they miss the opportunity that is before them, and the little they have invested is lost. However, if done right, a modest novice operation can make good money without going into debt for a fancy booth and equipment. At minimum, a large enough investment should be made to provide for a professional operation. Starting small with a minimal investment is a good way to get a sense of the business.

Here's a tip: Any extra investment you can afford should go toward good signs.

Then again, some folks might want to jump in with a large expensive operation. They buy a twenty foot manufactured trailer, equip it with stainless steel, and are then forced to buy a new one-ton truck just to haul it around. When their events don't produce the way they had envisioned, they may deeply regret the large monthly payments they are now making on their new equipment.

Here's the bottom line: In an established concession business, the larger your capital investment, the higher your return will be. However, the same does not hold true for new, non-established concessions. It may take several years to find and book enough good events to justify a large expensive operation. It might also take a year or two to learn what "busy" feels like, how to manage the logistics of "busy," and comfortably invest in and evolve into an operation capable of an ever-increasing volume of sales.

It would be unfair of me to suggest that you should start with a specific investment. Some people may have enough capital and expertise to dive into their first season with all the equipment they desire. Others will dip a toe in the shallow end, cautiously beginning with a minimal investment. It is unlikely that either party will reach their financial goals the first year. But both will likely make some money and gain valuable experience. The important things are to do enough research and planning to understand your personal and financial limitations and to balance that with an investment in your new business that is large enough to get the best start possible.

Operating Costs

The key to knowing whether or not you are making money, as well as setting prices, budgeting, and controlling costs, is to pay close attention to your operating costs. In this business, there are three types of operating costs. One is the *cost of goods*, which represents the actual dollar value of the products that you sell. Another type of operating costs is *event expenses*. These are expenses for things such as space fees, permit fees, fuel, propane, supplies, and helpers. Each of these expenses is directly related to each event. The third type of cost is *administrative overhead*. These are the basic costs of doing business for things such as maintenance, telephone, loan and interest payments, office supplies, and insurance.

Unlike a conventional business that is in operation year-round and whose operating costs remain somewhat constant during the course of the year, a concession has wildly fluctuating income and expenses. Many of the costs associated with operating a concession are realized well before the event season begins and before any money starts rolling in. Typical early expenses are: space fees, frequently paid at the time of application, pre-season maintenance expenses on vehicles and equipment, insurance premiums, and some permit fees. A successful concessionaire must be skilled at budgeting throughout the year in order to ensure enough revenue is available in the spring to pay all of the pre-season expenses. Once the season gets underway, the expenses associated with keeping the show on the road,

Yes, it is possible to open a concession for around five hundred dollars. Some event grounds have built-in facilities complete with kitchen appliances. For the cost of renting the facility, a health permit, and inventory, a person can be in business for at least the duration of the event. Nonprofits frequently take this approach for their yearly fundraiser. It is a good way for anyone to make some quick cash.

such as cost of goods, propane, fuel, and helpers' pay will be realized by each event.

Although all vendors have different overhead costs, on average, over the course of the summer, a typical vendor will spend fifty cents of every dollar they earn on operating costs. If your menu is priced too low relative to your product costs or you have unusually high maintenance expenses, that number can go higher.

Capital Reserves

The most easily overlooked aspect of starting a concession business is budgeting for adequate capital reserves. On a year-by-year basis, a vendor must have a very good idea of his or her personal living and spring start-up costs in order to budget for enough money to see through till the concession starts creating a solid stream of cash. Additionally, it is no coincidence that early season earnings are as unpredictable as the weather. In the spring, the weather is iffy, turnout is poor, and the operation is stiff and clumsy from sitting idle all winter. Most vendors won't see their bank accounts grow until the event season is well underway. If a financial calamity should occur before that time, such as suddenly needing major vehicle repairs, it would be crucial to have enough working capital available both to solve the problem and keep you afloat.

I hate to admit even to myself that the biggest drawback to the concession business is that, as much as I enjoy the end of the concession season, when I can put the trailer in mothballs, get caught up on yard work, take a little vacation, do some home improvement, and then kick back for the winter with a good book, the end of the season means no income. But one still needs to pay bills all winter. No matter how much money is deposited in the bank during the summer, without continuous income throughout the year, the balance gets drawn down. Over the span of a career, it is very hard to increase one's net worth if most of the money earned in the summer gets spent paying bills in the winter. It's true: Many concessionaires make enough during the season to live on the entire year. Yes, they have kids in college and own their homes. What they do to make it work is budget carefully and use the winter months productively.

Now, consider another perspective. There are many full-time, underpaid wage earners who have dreams of owning their own businesses but not enough spare time or money to pursue their dreams. Living on the financial edge without hope of an opportunity to try for a better life, these folks are in a far more precarious financial position. Concessionaires have opportunity to grow their financial estate continually by partnering this business with another worthwhile and fulfilling enterprise. Or they can do what many concessionaires do: Take the concession south for the winter where they earn an income with the concession year-round.

Working Capital and Capital Reserves Worksheet

Living Expenses			Pre/Early Season Expenses			Mid Season Expenses	
Expense	Monthly	Yearly	Expense	$	Month	Expense	$
Mortgage/Rent			Space Fees			On Going Maintenance	
Utilities			Equip. Maintenance			Product/Supplies	
Groceries			Vehicle Maintenance			Fuel	
Insurance			Business Insurance			Labor	
Taxes			Health Permits			Propane	
Repair & Maintenance			DMV Licensing			Health Permits	
Medical			Telephone				
Auto			Product/Supplies (2 events)				
Fuel							
IRA Contribution							
Loan Payment							
Entertainment							
Gifts/Seasonal							
Totals							

Income	$	Month
Total Income		

Accurate forecasting is important in planning for adequate start-up capital and capital reserves. This basic worksheet will get you started.

Start-up Costs Worksheet

Booth (Concession trailer, tent, pushcart)   _____

_____

_____

Vehicles (RV, truck, stock trailer)   _____

_____

_____

Major Equipment (deep fryers, grill, freezers)   _____

_____

_____

Minor Equipment (warming tray, cash register, ice chests)   _____

_____

_____

Misc. Equipment (hand truck, lights, step stool)   _____

_____

_____

Insurance (business liability, vehicle)   _____

_____

_____

Space Fees (each event)   _____

_____

_____

Licenses (health permits)   _____

_____

_____

Starting Inventory (first event)   _____

_____

_____

Operating Capital (goods and overhead reserves)   _____

_____

_____

Capital Reserves (personal living costs reserves) $_____

This is a brief example of the expenses you will need to consider when calculating your start-up costs. It is by no means inclusive.

Part 3

Events and
Venues

CHAPTER 9

Analyzing an Event's Potential for Profit

Types of Events

In my mind, most events fall into one of two categories, fairs or festivals. The main difference between the two is in the way they are organized. There are also many events that don't fit into these two categories, such as, auctions, sporting events, and bazaars. For the purposes of this book, when I mention festivals, I am referring to small community events, though in fact some festivals rival regional fairs for size and cost. No matter the venue, the process of finding, screening, and acquiring booth space is basically the same for each.

Fairs

Fairs are county, regional, or state-sponsored events. They are largely organized by salaried professionals who must answer to a fair board, which in turn must answer to the county commissioner or some other government entity. Most receive government funding. As you can imagine, they are very political, expensive, and often difficult for vendors to get into. But the earning potential can be huge. Large, high-volume concession operations depend on large regional fairs to justify their business. Concessionaires with adequate capital, equipment, capacity, and employees can earn upwards of thirty thousand dollars at one of these events, more than many small operations earn in an entire season. However, because of the high cost to participate, they are extremely risky. The space fees at most *county* fairs are determined as a percentage of gross sales. By contrast, the vendors at large *regional* and *state* fairs often bid for vendor space on a three-year contract. Sometimes these spaces go for as high as fifty thousand dollars for each of those three years. Ouch! These events can run two to four weeks long and are frequently dominated by fast food conglomerates. Not all fairs are large, and, in fact, many small county fairs have the appearance and atmosphere of a small community festival. Small county fairs are less commercialized. Everyone knows everyone else, and the entire community may participate in one way or another. Youth organizations like 4H and FFA (Future Farmers of America) are the backbone of rural county fairs. Unfortunately, over the past few years, this strong youth presence has been declining.

Here's a tip: During fairs, 4H and FFA kids stay on the fairgrounds to care for and show their livestock. While there, they purchase nearly all of their meals from food booths. On the first day of the fair, if your food doesn't pass their scrutiny, you will get very little business from the kids for the duration of the fair. This is one of the most important first impressions you will ever make in the business.

Festivals

Festivals are community events. Nearly every community, large or small, has some type of festival during the year. They are usually organized and supported by a volunteer civic group, local government, or private organization. Not all festivals are small events. In fact, some festivals are even larger and more expensive than many county fairs. Some festivals are organized for the benefit of the entire community whereas others may have a single attraction aimed at one specific demographic.

A small town festival.

There are thousands of events held each year, and no two are the same. Events held in neighboring communities with the same line-up of activities, similar locations, and identical attendance may prove to have very different sales results. A variety of variables at each event will greatly influence the success of each vendor. Additionally, anything that affects the sales of your competitor, for good or bad, will, in turn, affect yours as well. Never are all of these elements known by you prior to doing the event. So, how do you go about selecting the best events? The practical approach is to consider and weigh the various known factors, make some generalizations, and hope for the best.

Over the years, I have come to make my own generalizations about various indicators of what may or may not influence the profitability of an event. Remember: These are just generalizations based on my experiences in this part of the country. I am as frequently surprised or disappointed by some of the new events that I select as is any vendor.

I apologize for the stereotyping in these generalizations. In truth, I find it a little amusing that although you might think there is a general mix of all sorts of people in every community and at every event, the truth is actually the opposite. Every community and every event has its own unique character. Additionally, certain types of events draw certain types of people. It's the unique character of each event that makes this business so fun.

Attractions and Activities

An event is not an event unless there are some activities that attract people to attend. In large part, it's the activities that also determine how long people will stay. It's not enough for people to show up. There must also be something there to keep the crowd amused for an extended period of time. As vendors, we want the crowd to come to eat lunch and dinner and then stay for dessert.

- *Parades* are frequently held in conjunction with a festival on Saturday morning. They are usually a huge draw for the entire town. Immediately following the parade, the crowd will surge to the event to check out the activities and to eat.

- *Carnivals* are a good draw for families and kids. A carnival will usually extend the people's stay late into the evening.

- *Craft booths* are a small but important draw and are always a nice addition to an event. The more crafts, the better. They en-

Here's a tip: The sole purpose of certain festivals is to raise money for local nonprofit organizations. When vendors inquire into participating, they are told that the event is for nonprofit organizations only. However, as a professional vendor, you may still be able to participate by offering to sponsor and to donate a portion of your proceeds to a specific nonprofit organization. Personally, I love the concept of people gathering to celebrate and support their favorite charities. As a member of my favorite organization, I appreciate the large audience of an event to raise both money and awareness for its cause. With my organization's banner hung from my booth, I proudly provide good food as I hand out leaflets of information provided by the organization.

courage a crowd to stay at least as long as it takes to browse through the craft booths.

- *Art festivals* draw a crowd with discriminating taste. Paired with wine and music, they can be a very good attraction.

- *Stage entertainment*, such as amateur music, talent shows, dog shows, and karaoke, are small attractions at large events and large attractions at small events. In small communities, local talent is much more popular than professional entertainment because everyone likes to watch people they know performing on stage.

- *Rodeos* are a tough sale. From the viewpoint of a bored concessionaire, the people that attend rodeos are prone to act like cattle, filing into the event as if herded, barely stopping to eat, then stampeding out in the direction of the beer garden when the rodeo is over. Unless the rodeo is paired with other activities, such as a carnival, they are a difficult place to make money.

- *Timber carnivals* are probably popular only in the Northwest. They are a good draw because people will wander in and out of the grounds to eat.

- *Music festivals* draw different kinds of people, depending on the type of music. They can draw a very good crowd. It's your call if your menu and ears are suited to the type of music and participants.

- *Flea/open air markets* are fun and, if big enough, can draw a steady stream of new faces past your booth all day long.

- *Special events* such as horse shows, tractor pulls, antique shows, dog shows, sporting events, renaissance fairs, and so on, are better judged individually and by attendance/booth ratio.

- *Beer gardens* are an indication that the event will last into the evening. However, if the beer garden is the only event in the evening, don't be fooled into thinking that it will generate a lot of sales. Unless you have a high tolerance for serving inebriated customers, it's usually not worth the hassle.

- *Wine tasting* customers, on the other hand, will generally remain active and friendly participants in the event.

- *Unusual competitions* are a huge draw and can literally put a town on the map. I have participated in events with contests like slug races, rooster crowing, and manly man competitions, all of which were hugely successful and great fun.

As strange as it may sound, most coordinators are reluctant to tap into the vast collective experience of the participating vendors by asking for activity ideas. Unfortunately, many events are struggling, and, but for a few creative ideas from vendors, could really turn the corner toward a successful event.

Attendance/Booth Ratio

In some cases, you can do the math to help determine if the event is likely to be profitable. In simple terms, if at a well-attended event yours were the only food booth, you would likely have it made. Of course, in reality, that rarely happens. Nor-

One event I attend has a talent contest for young people where the local business community collectively donates a five hundred dollar cash award for each age group in the competition. The kids prepare their acts all year. The event is three days of excited anticipation, which ends with a show of talent that is remarkable.

mally, there are many variables, such as your competition and space location, which will also influence your share of sales. If you learn the expected attendance and the expected number of food booths, you can roughly determine your share of business. If you learn what the other booths are selling, better yet. For example, at a given event, you might learn that the expected attendance is about five thousand people. Out of twelve food booths, six are selling main course meals, one of which is the same menu as yours. Four are selling sweets and candy. One is selling espresso, and one is selling popcorn. After adjusting your calculations for known factors, such as your space location, you can roughly determine where you might fit into the equation. After experiencing a variety of events, you will learn how well your menu competes with other particular menus. You will also learn who the other vendors are and how well your booth can compete with their specific operations. You should also know that trying to determine the quality of an event by "counting heads" is not at all a perfect science. In fact, it's not science at all and is only good for estimating the possibilities.

Event coordinators frequently have an inclination to "sell real estate," meaning they overbook their events with food booths. In effect, they are cutting the pie into critically tiny pieces. There are several likely reasons a coordinator will do this. First and most obviously, the more food booths that attend, the more space fees the event collects. Although some event coordinators don't intend to overbook and, in fact, may tell you they have a policy to limit booths, they simply cannot say no when vendors call to inquire. Another reason they overbook may be to create the impression that the event is successful. Certainly, the more booths at an event, the larger and more successful an event appears. Some coordinators overbook because they hate to see customers standing in line. They don't realize that food booths must have a line of customers for at least part of the time to make any money. There needs to be a balance. A large crowd with too few booths is not good for the crowd or the event. A small crowd with too many booths is not good for the vendors.

Event Location

The event location may not influence your sales as much as it will influence the level of difficulty to participate. For example, an event held in a large, grassy park will usually provide plenty of room for you to maneuver while setting up and lots of elbow room while you work. Grass also provides an enjoyable place for the attendees to play on and relax. On the other hand, a street fair can be a difficult location. Obstructions, such as telephone poles, curbs, and buildings, can make setting up difficult. The attendees will not be inclined to loiter when the asphalt is hot. Some street fairs have a difficult time arranging for power and water for the vendors. Be cautious of events that are spread throughout a town. If the carnival is located in a parking lot on main street but the craft and food booths are set up across town at the school, the crowd will not congregate in one area for long. Most county fairgrounds are designed with vendors in mind. There are plenty of power and water hookups, plenty of toilets, and frequently even shower facilities.

Event Duration

It may seem obvious that an event held for one day will not generate as much business as one held for three. This may be true in most cases, but at nearly all events, certain days of the event are better than others. If you do an event that is scheduled for four days but the attendance is barely noticeable until Saturday, you have invested three days of time, propane, possibly wasted product, and wages for very little return. On the other hand, a good five-day event will almost certainly have a higher return than a good three-day event. Some events have limited hours, ending in the afternoon, whereas others continue late into the evening. Sales made during the dinner hour are dollars that add up quickly.

Space Fees

In the old days, the space fee was referred to in "carnival speak" as "the nut." Back then, the carnival would roll into town seeking supplies from local merchants on the promise that the tab would be paid when the show ended and the carnival was flush with cash. Instead, on the last day of the show, the carnival would sneak off during the night. So, angry merchants began to each take a lug nut off a carnival wagon wheel to hold as collateral until the bill was paid.

Here's more "carnival speak":

Fin: five buck

Sawbuck: ten bucks

Double: twenty bucks

Yard note: one hundred bucks

Slough (pronounced like cow): tear down equipment

Joint: booth

Call: opening time

Draw: cash advance

Flat Fees

These days, the majority of small community festivals charge the space fee as a flat fee based on the frontage length of your booth. A standard flat fee is usually charged for each increment of ten feet. If your booth is fifteen feet, they may charge you for two whole spaces, or they may charge you for one space, plus an additional amount for each foot over ten feet. Most vendors prefer a flat fee to a percentage fee. They like to know what the space fee will cost before committing to the event. They can decide upfront if the price is worth the risk of bombing out as weighed against the potential rewards if the event is successful. A flat fee event is nearly always less expensive than a percentage fee event.

Percentage Fees

Fairs and large urban events are more apt to charge a minimum fee against a percentage of gross sales. What this means is that an initial minimum fee is required as a deposit, usually paid early on when the contract is offered. Then, at the end of each day of the event, your daily gross sales are recorded. At the end of the event, you are required to pay a percentage of your total gross sales, minus the initial fee and minus any sales taxes collected. A percentage fee generally ranges anywhere from 10 to 25 percent. This is all spelled out in a contract. Event contracts vary, so be careful to study the terms. Also, be certain of the amount of space you are buying. For example, a contract might state that each ten-foot space requires a $250 deposit. However, the small print may say that if your booth is twenty feet long, only a single deposit of $250 will be credited against your percentage of gross sales.

> Here's a tip: Unlike most other contracts, a vendor contract is not negotiable.

Food vendors generally resent paying a fee as high as 20 percent of gross sales. They argue that forty to sixty cents of every dollar they bring in is already going toward covering expenses. An event that charges a fee of 20 percent of *gross sales* may in fact be receiving half of the booth's profit. Vendors will argue that a percentage of *net sales*, revenue after event expenses are deducted, would be much more fair. Unfortunately, events never allow the vendors to subtract the event expenses before calculating the space fee. It hardly seems fair when you consider that it is the concessionaire who is doing all of the work, shouldering the risk, and also paying a percentage on money that has been spent on wages, licenses, and fuel. With this line of thinking, it is very tempting to "skim" by deliberately neglecting to ring every sale into the cash register, thereby hiding some of the sales from the event. Event organizers are very wise to this trick. Not only are they skilled at having a pretty good idea how much business you're doing just by watching your booth, but also some have actually been known to have "spotters" out watching each booth for signs of deception.

On the other hand, some vendors prefer to pay a percentage rather than a flat fee. There is comfort in knowing that if sales are poor, your space fee will not be so high. They also argue that by paying the event a percentage, they are giving the event a stake in the food booths' success. In this case, it is in the organizers' best interests to do the best they can to ensure the success of the food booths. Unfortunately, this fact is apparently lost on many coordina-

> I know of a case where the spotters shut down a booth for skimming when in fact the cashier was simply making change for someone who needed to use a pay phone.

tors. There are many events that make no effort to support the vendors and, in fact, seem to adopt policies that undermine the efforts of the concessionaires to maximize sales.

Some food vendors consider an event a competition. Egos are at stake. Also, a high grossing booth that pays an honest percentage to the event is much more apt to be given special consideration for booth space the following year.

Booking a small operation into an event with a high space fee may not be feasible. A booth that has a limited sales capacity simply cannot make the numbers work to warrant doing a high-volume, high-expense event. Average-size vendors generally prefer to do average, reasonably priced three-day community events rather than larger, high-volume, and more expensive county fairs. Although your sales may be higher at a large event, when you factor in the additional cost of additional employees, longer hours, additional product and propane, and high space fees, your net profit at the end of the event might not make it relatively worthwhile.

Let's compare the gross and net sales of two events. Each event is four days long and costs the same for the health permit, stock, fuel, and wages. For space fees, one event charges a $300 flat rate whereas the other charges 15 percent of gross sales. The sales figures are the same on each day for both events. These figures were taken from an actual flat-fee event that has been considering switching to percentage.

Flat Rate Event		15% of Gross Sales Event	
Sales			
Thursday	$745		$745
Friday	1495		1495
Saturday	3911		3911
Sunday	675		675
Total Sales	**6826**		**6826**
Space Fee	$300	(6826@15%)	$1024
Health Permit	75		75
Fuel	100		100
Stock	1500		1500
Wages	400		400
Total Expenses	**2375**		**3099**
Profit	**$4451**		**$3727**

Booking the flat-fee event instead of the percentage event puts an extra $724 in your pocket. On the other hand, if sales only totaled $3,413, half as much for the four days, then the space fee for the percentage event would be $512. The flat-fee would still be a better event by over $200. And if the sales were $13,652, double for the four days, the space fee would be $2,048. That's $1,748 more in your pocket from the flat-fee event than the percentage event. It appears that there is not much likelihood that the percentage event would ever be the better deal.

So, why do vendors select, much less seek out, percentage events when they appear to be such a bad deal? In fact, large events that charge a percentage of gross sales are a critical venue for concessions with the capacity to generate upwards of $10,000 in sales over a three- or four-day event. The only events that have an attendance high enough to affect this level of sales are large events. Large events are big business for everyone involved. They cost a lot of money to produce, and big bucks are expected to be the reward. The event managers don't monkey around with small space fees. They are trying to make money, and they know their event is worth a bundle to vendors in potential sales. So, if you want to earn big bucks from your concession, you must be willing to operate a high-volume operation and pay high space fees. If you only attend small community events that charge a flat fee, you won't be exposed to enough potential customers to generate a large number of sales.

Don't get me wrong. Small concessionaires do attend some percentage events. When weighing several event options, sometimes the county fair with a percentage space fee will be a better choice. With higher attendance and longer business hours, it may produce more sales than other event options. For example:

	Flat Rate Event		**15% of Gross Sales Event**
Sales			
Thursday	$300		$745
Friday	800		1495
Saturday	1500		3911
Sunday	300		675
Total Sales	**2900**		**6826**
Space Fee	$300	(6826@15%)	$1024
Health Permit	75		75
Fuel	100		100
Stock	500		1500
Wages	200		400
Total Expenses	**1175**		**3099**
Profit	**$1725**		**$3727**

In this example, the percentage event had the same number of sales as the earlier example, but sales at the flat-fee event were poor. Even with lower expenses for stock and wages and undoubtedly less work and stress, the flat-fee event was less than half as prosperous as the percentage event. These figures are taken from actual events.

Script

There are a few events that, along with charging a percentage of gross sales for space fees, also require that customers pay with script rather than cash. Just like buying a book of tickets at Disneyland, attendees buy a book of script in a choice of denominations when they enter the grounds and use the tickets to make their purchases while at the event. At the conclusion of the event, vendors turn in the script they earned in exchange for cash, minus their space fee. I can only assume that the main reason that event coordinators do this is because it makes it impossible for vendors to skim when it's time to pay up.

Event Admission

Some events are free to the public. Others charge the public to park and then charge them again for admission. There's no doubt, it costs a lot of money to organize an event, and the money must come from somewhere. Frequently, it's the large expensive events charging admission that also charge the vendors a high fee. This, in turn, causes the vendors to raise their prices to help cover their expenses. The net effect of all this is that the public gets cranky. The public can understand and accept the cost of parking and admission, but it doesn't understand why it's being charged three bucks for a corn dog when one can buy them at the corner market for fifty cents.

I once participated in a script event. At the close of the event, instead of manually counting the script, the coordinators weighed it to calculate its value. Their method cost me several hundred dollars. Needless to say, I did not return the following year.

This whole cycle of big bucks and crankiness creates an atmosphere that can be less than pleasant to work in. More importantly, however, money spent by the public on parking and admission is less money that will be spent at a food booth. Admission can also influence the number of attendees. Members of a community are not likely to attend an event more than once if they are charged at the gate.

Event Age

The number of years that an event has been running is usually, though not always, an indication of its quality. An event takes time to establish, work out kinks, develop a reputation, and create a following before it can become well organized and well attended. This is not, however, always the case. The longest running fair in my state has the reputation as the worst fair for vendors. Be cautious of new events that are organized by a single or small group of people that has no sponsorship to help pay for advertising and promotion. An event so handicapped has little potential. However, getting in on the ground floor of a fledgling event could pay off down the road. You will pat yourself on the back when you have seniority and a prime space location at an event that other vendors would now give their right arm to get into.

Event Organization

In this business, there are not too many things as pleasant as working at an event that is well managed, where the coordinators treat the vendors with respect and as a welcomed and appreciated part of the event community. Unfortunately, the least recognized and appreciated contributor to event quality is the group of volunteer organizers. Some communities have a large population of civic-minded individuals who pull together year after year. Often, for both the public and the vendors, these are the best events to attend. Other communities mostly leave the burden of organization to a handful of generous individuals who rapidly burn out, causing the event to find fresh coordinators the following year. New coordinators come in fresh and excited with new ideas, only to burn out and go the way of their predecessor.

Coordinator/Vendor Relationship

In many ways, our ability to earn a living is in the hands of the event coordinators. It is they who permit us to participate in the event, determine our location, and how many competitors we will have. It is up to them to arrange for the necessities of electrical power and water, schedule the entertainment and promotions, arrange parking for our stock vehicles, and to see to every minute detail of the event. In one way or another, every one of the hundreds of decisions they make will impact vendors and influence the level of our success. They also have the final word. Their cooperation or lack of cooperation with the participating vendors can make the difference between an event that is enjoyable and prosperous and one that we plan never to attend again. Whether we like it or not, even if we do everything right in our business, the skill and cooperation of the coordinators and the quality of our relationship with them will still have a tremendous impact on our business. This relationship starts from the first moment you make contact on the phone.

In my experience, most coordinators, fair boards, and event committees are sincere in their efforts and cooperative with the vendors. However, very few have had the experience of being a professional concessionaire and gained the perspective that comes with it. All coordinators are different. Some are quite honest and secure in their knowledge that we vendors are easily replaced. After all, they receive inquiries from possibly hundreds of vendors each year looking for events. Others are eager to do what they can to help us succeed and to encourage us to return to their event each year. Unfortunately, too many coordinators don't grasp the fact that this is a business. A lot of money and our livelihoods are at stake. Most concessionaires would like to conduct their business relationships in a businesslike fashion. However, the prevalent attitude of many coordinators makes this nearly impossible. Many event organizers are simply not prepared or willing to participate in any kind of honest discourse. The worst offenders are the very large and expensive events where upwards of hundreds of thousands of dollars may be at stake. These events rightfully have their rules and policies. But, rather than have open dialogue with vendors, a vendor must simply submit or not be welcomed to participate. In fact, it is at these large events, where a vendor is required to sign a contract that the least amount of discourse occurs. Unlike other contractual business arrangements, the vendor is rarely offered an opportunity to discover what they will receive in exchange for their contractual commitment. In most cases, a contract is offered, and the vendor can either accept it at face value or not.

In defense of the coordinators, most events are beleaguered by a host of logistical complications, from committees wrought with egos and politics to physical obstacles, event site limitations, and uncooperative local property owners, just to name a few. Additionally, coordinators are besieged with commentary and complaints from participating vendors, all of whom have special needs, opinions, and varying levels of professionalism. It's no wonder that coordinators lose patience with the whole affair and become antagonistic and uncooperative.

I view the booking of an event as what should be considered a short-term business partnership between the event and myself. The event provides the vendor a venue to do business, and the vendor provides a service and financial support to the event. Each party should be willing to be honest and forthright with the other party. Influential statistics and information should be freely given, and each party should have an obligation to fulfill their commitment and do the right thing for the common good. Many coordinators do not realize that if they do a

> If you happen to attend an event where the coordinator asks for feedback and ideas, be as artfully tactful as you can. Not only is good diplomacy always the best approach for its own merits but also because the opportunity to provide input is rare. Why squander the opportunity to share ideas by choosing that moment to vent your grievances?

good job, treat the vendors fairly, and provide us a fair opportunity for profit, we would return year after year. This is a benefit to them. Veteran vendors learn the drill at each event. We also usually know each other well enough to work as a team. This makes the coordinator's job easier. The event runs smoother with veteran vendors. Further, the attendees love the familiarity of buying their favorite treats from their favorite concessions year after year. This, in turn, promotes attendance and is hugely beneficial to everyone involved.

CHAPTER 10

Event Scheduling
Know-How

Finding Good Events

Establishing a schedule of good events is a long process. Not only does every vendor go through the process, but also the process never ends. In the beginning, a start-up concession needs to pursue possible venues actively to develop the new business. Vendors can refer to the usual event guides and publications, contact local venues and fairgrounds, or call the chamber of commerce. Researching possible events takes a lot of time and effort, as does making contact with coordinators, submitting appropriate paperwork, and following up with confirmation. Even after more than twenty years in the business, I still spend the spring trying to find and schedule good events to replace certain events that were disappointing the prior season. Events change over time. An event at which you have been doing well for several years may experience a slow decline, perhaps due to a failing local economy. A steady decline in sales might cause you to give up an event to find a different one for that date the following year. It's more common, however, for an event to undergo a drastic change. Perhaps the new coordinator decides to fix an event that, in our view, isn't broken. The coordinator might move the event to a new location or charge admission after a long tradition of being a free event. These types of changes, though sometimes necessary, will nearly always adversely impact attending vendor's sales.

157

A vendor's first year in the concession business is by far the most difficult. Not only are you learning the business from scratch, but you're also doing an entire season of events totally blind. You have no way of knowing what to expect when you arrive at a new event or how it will play out. In fact, even experienced vendors find it difficult to do an event for the first time. Even if you ask the coordinator all the right questions, the truth won't be revealed until after the event gets underway. There are hundreds of variables that will impact your business and no way to determine what those factors will be in advance of actually doing the event. On your first visit, you won't know how much product to bring, what the booth layout and obstacles are, what time to expect to get busy, who your competitors are, how well it's organized, and much more. Your first visit to an event is always an introductory trial. Your second visit, when you attend with the correct amount of stock and preparation, is when the actual job of getting down to making sales begins. Event scheduling also gets easier each year. Your own experience, as well as information you get from talking with other vendors, will help determine which events to do and which ones to stay away from.

Here's a tip: Be prudent when talking about events with other vendors. What may be a bad event for one vendor may be a good event for another.

Prime event season for much of the country runs roughly from Memorial Day to Labor Day. In the warm southern states, the event season may be the reverse or even go all year long. In the northern states, planning an event schedule for the season usually starts in February and takes several months. Many small, volunteer-run events don't start their planning until late spring. Rather than risk being too late, it is better to start calling the coordinators early. You can always check back with them later when they are more organized. County fairs start their planning anytime from December to February. They first offer space to the previous year's vendors before offering new vendors an opportunity to fill a vacancy. Really large events may even contract their vendors twelve months in advance.

Good events often allow only a limited number of food booths. They can be difficult to get into because previous vendors return year after year. It doesn't hurt to apply each year because you never know when a space will become available to you. It's important to start your event booking activities early. Most good events have their vendors locked in with contracts several months in advance of the date of the event.

Event Listings

There are many ways to learn about events, their dates, and contact numbers in your area:

- *Contact your state department of tourism.* Request a copy of the annual state calendar of events. Every state issues this free booklet. It is an extensive, though not complete list of events, the communities in which they are held, dates, and contact numbers. It is a staple source of event information for vendors of all types.

- *Search the Internet for websites of event-listing publications.* Many can be found by searching keywords, such as crafters, markets, events, food booths, food concession, etc. I have made a list in the appendix of a few listings I was quickly able to find.

- *Check the website of your regional fair association.*

- *Check the website of local counties for a listing of county events.*

- *Contact the chamber of commerce of any community for a listing of community events.*

- *Contact the county fairgrounds for a list of events that are scheduled at their facility.*

- *Talk with other food vendors.* Although most vendors are very secretive about good events that they currently attend, they may have knowledge of other events that are worthwhile.

- *Watch your local newspaper for upcoming events.* Many small events are listed only in the newspaper a week or two before the event date. If they haven't already arranged for food, they may be happy to hear from you. Though large events have likely already made food booth arrangements, a note in your notebook will remind you to check with them earlier next year.

- *Be imaginative.* Many special interest groups sponsor unpublished events that attract large numbers of people. Many do not have food available on-site for the participants and may be thrilled to have you cater their event. You might go in as a vendor and donate a percentage of sales to the club or act as a caterer and serve a set amount of dishes for a fee. A good place to learn of associations is to visit your local library or chamber of commerce. They will likely have a reference book of association listings. Or you can contact local sport clubs, horse academies, dog clubs, radio control clubs, motorcycle clubs, etc.

- *Contact local carnival companies.* Many will contract with independent food concessionaires on a per event or per season basis. They typically charge 25 to 30 percent of gross sales.

Start by sitting down with a calendar, a pencil, a notebook, and a list of events in your targeted area. A day planner is a very handy tool for keeping notes, phone numbers, and your schedule organized. Highlight or make a list of the events, dates, and contacts of potential events. Then start dialing. Be prepared to take copious notes. Invariably, when you call, no one will answer the phone, you will get an answering machine, or the number provided will no longer be valid. If you run into a dead end, call the chamber of commerce. They are usually helpful at knowing about events planned in their community. Keep track of the date and results of all of your contacting efforts from start to finish. You will probably have to follow up on each one. When you do finally contact the people who are coordinating the event, the first thing you need to know is if they are accepting applications for food vendors. If they say yes, you are halfway there. The rest of the conversation will be a series of questions and answers on both sides. They may ask you what you are selling and what type and size of booth you have. You, however, will have a long list of questions for them. Keep notes. The answers to these questions will help you choose the event with the best opportunity for profit. I've made a list of some of the questions you may want to ask the coordinator. I will go into more detail on these subjects later in the chapter.

- Verify the date of the event. It is not uncommon for the date in a listing to be inaccurate.

- What type of attractions and activities are planned? It's the attractions that persuade people to attend. Some attractions are more persuasive than others.

- Where is the event held? Is it held in a park, on the street, in a parking lot, at a fairgrounds, etc.

- How accessible is the area? Nearly all food booths require a certain amount of space to operate efficiently. Most vendors store a stock vehicle or have cases of product behind their booths. Others may need a specific amount of room just to maneuver their vehicles. Whatever your specific space needs are, be sure to find out in advance if the event can provide you the room you need.

- How many people are expected to attend?

- How many vendors will be invited to participate? Are any of them returning from the previous year?

- Does the event have a policy of limiting duplicating menus?

- Will another vendor be selling your specific menu? Small events may sometimes be willing to tell you what the other scheduled vendors are selling.

- How much is the space fee?

- Will electricity and water be available?

- Is parking available for extra vehicles?

- What day and time do vendors set up?

- During what hours will the event be open?

- Will the public be charged for admission or parking?

If what you hear over the phone sounds promising, ask the coordinator to send you an application. Sometimes, even after asking a lot of questions and looking carefully at several applications, it is still very hard to choose the right event. In that case, you might want to consider any other factors that could impact the event. The condition of the local economy, the nearest population base, likeliness of good weather, and nearby events competing for the same attendees on the same day can also influence the quality of an event. If you're still stumped, you might just choose the event that is the least expensive, the most convenient, or that looks to be the most fun.

> Here's a tip: Anytime a coordinator appears overly eager for you to attend, it may be a signal that the event is having a hard time keeping vendors. The probable reason is that previous vendors were unable to make enough profit.

It is very unwise to try to book into large fairs until after you have gotten some experience at several small community festivals. It's only by practicing at small events that you will learn the amount of stock you will go through, how to operate your business efficiently, and how to tackle the hundreds of logistical difficulties that arise. It takes an experienced vendor to risk the high expense of large events and be able to pull it off with a healthy profit.

The Event Contract Application Process

Nearly all fairs and most large festivals have an Internet site that you can visit to learn almost everything you need to know about the event. The site will give you the entertainment schedule, prices for booth space, deadlines for application, contact numbers, and an application for you to print out on your computer. These sites provide enough information that you can screen an event without wasting the time and money of a long distance call to the coordinator. For events that interest you, even if you get all the information you need from the website, you may still want to call the coordinator for more current and less generic information. It's also important to develop a business relationship with the coordinator, which usually starts with a phone conversation.

County and regional fairs don't generally require that a fee be paid with the application but instead require a deposit be paid when a contract is offered and signed. If that is the case, you should maximize your chances of being offered a contract by sending applications to as many fairs as you can. Smaller, flat-fee events do require the fee to be paid with the application. Although your check will be returned if you are not accepted into the event, you may decide to apply only to one event for each date. Otherwise, you run the risk of becoming double booked. Most coordinators will simply consider your application approved and cash your check without any further communication with you. At that point, it is up to you to cancel the event you choose not to attend, then wait and hope to be reimbursed for your space fee.

Almost all applications ask for the size of your booth. Although most space fees are determined by the length of your booth, don't be tempted to claim less than you actually need. Even though you may hate to pay for your tongue length, the fact is, it's made of steel and can't be ignored when it comes time to squeeze your booth into your space. At small events, many festival coordinators will try to accommodate a vendor who fudged by squeezing him or her into the space of the neighboring vendor. In my humble opinion, rather than unfairly force an innocent vendor to forfeit some space, the correct approach would be for the offending vendor to for-

> Here's a tip: When scheduling an event, keep a close eye on the date the event is open to the public as well as the set-up and tear-down dates. It is important to allow enough time between events to clean, stock up on supplies, travel, and set up. During fair season, one fair may end on Sunday evening and another start on Tuesday morning.

feit the event, which would be the likely outcome if you fudge your space at a large fair.

While filling out an application for an event, pay particular attention to the booth space dimensions. Some events, fairs in particular, are very strict in their measurements whereas others are much more casual. Some events provide a walkway between booths. Others do not. This is one of the many particulars of the event that you won't learn until you get there. I recommend that you scrutinize the application and ask questions. For instance, suppose the application indicates that each 10′ x 10′ space costs $250. Now, suppose that your booth is a 10′ x 10′ tent. Perfect. But wait. You also need your propane bottles to set next to your tent. You also like to have room to walk around to the front of your booth so you can clean your front counter. Additionally, you need your 16′-stock trailer set up behind your tent. What do you do? You call the coordinator to learn how much, if any, space is allowed behind the booths for stock vehicles. You also ask how much space will be allowed between booths. If there are acres of open space behind your booth, the stock trailer should not be a problem. If the coordinator plans to provide plenty of space between booths, your propane bottles and personal walk space, again, should not be a problem. Pay your $250 for your 10′ x 10′ space. On the other hand, if there is not much room behind the booth space and no walkways will be provided between the booths, you may want to buy a 20′-space. With a 20′-space you will have room to keep your stock trailer either behind or next to your tent. In either case, you would also have enough elbow room to access your front counter. It is important to communicate honestly about your space needs prior to committing to an event. It is also important that the coordinator is honest with you. No concessionaire enjoys being shoehorned into a space because of poor planning. Nor do coordinators appreciate a vendor who shows up with a booth that is larger than what was stated on the application.

Follow the instructions on the application. Strangely, most applications will offer very little information about the event, particularly the planned schedule of activities. A schedule of event activities is important to new vendors. It helps determine an event's potential for profit. It also tells them when the booths may get busy so they can be prepared. What little information they do offer is often printed on the same form as the application, which you will be sending back to them. Make a copy of your completed application to keep for your records. Also, make a note of the date you returned the application, how much you paid, the size of the space you paid for, whether an insurance certificate is enclosed or needed by a certain deadline, the set-up date and time, and the county in which the event will be held.

Some events will send you a confirmation notice that you have been accepted into their event, along with vendor information and parking passes. Others will send you nothing—in which case your canceled check should be confirmation enough. However, to be certain that you are indeed expected at the event, confirm your space with the coordinator early on. As you send in applications, if you do not get a response from an event within a reasonable period of time, you may want to call to confirm whether or not your application was received. Many event coordinators are slow to assign booth spaces and notify the vendors who will not be attending. Unfortunately, each day that you wait for a response reduces your chances of finding an alternative event if this one should fall through.

As you receive confirmation for your events, mark them into your calendar. It is a good idea to develop a file system to keep all of your paperwork organized. You will always want to know the status of each event and of you permit application, to be sure you have all your "ducks lined up" when you arrive at the event. (See Appendix 2 for sample event applications.)

Your Promotional Brochure

Your promotional flyer is an important tool for promoting your business to prospective events. By educating coordinators with a flyer or brochure about your business, you not only increase your odds of getting a contract, but also you enable them to make plans for the best possible situation for you when you get there. This is the place to tell them about your operational needs and to give them answers to questions about your business that they don't think to ask on the application. Your promotional material should be included with your application. If you have access to a computer, you can easily design an attractive document that introduces your business, describes your menu, outlines any needs you have, such as water and power, and diagrams the dimensions and configuration of your booth. If you can provide photos, even better. If you have a concession trailer, tell them where the service window and tongue are located. Most event coordinators will measure out and assign spaces before everyone arrives with their various booths. If they understand in advance your booth's configuration, they will be better able to allow you enough room to set up and operate comfortably. Photos of your attractive booth may inspire them to give you a more visible location. If you don't yet have photos, do a drawing. The more information the coordinator has about your operation, the less likely you both will be disappointed by unpleasant surprises when you arrive. (See Appendix 2 for an example of a promotional flyer.)

Health Permit Applications

After you make some progress filling in your calendar of scheduled events, you will want to call each of the county health departments in which you will be working to request an application for a temporary restaurant permit. Many health departments have deadlines for when they must receive your application. Along with the application, they will send you a list of basic licensing requirements. In the event that a health department has a requirement that is unique to its county, you will want to be informed as soon as possible so you can take what steps may be required in order to comply.

Temporary restaurant permit applications are generally fairly straightforward. Some are one page of simple questions about you, your booth, and your menu. Others are several pages long and additionally ask for a diagram of your booth and the specifics of your food handling procedure. Fees vary from county to county and can range between five dollars and one hundred and forty dollars for one event. Some counties will return to you a receipt or a signed copy of your license prior to the event. Others will wait to inspect your booth before they give you a copy. (See Appendix 2 for a sample Health Permit Application and a Health Department Guidelines Graphic).

Liability Insurance Certificates

Some events require the vendors to provide a certificate of insurance naming the event and specified parties as "additionally insured." This is simply a document confirming your policy and coverage and additionally covers the named party under your policy for the date of the event. As you complete your event schedule for the season, make a list of the events requiring an insurance certificate, the language that is used to name the "additionally insured," and the address where it should be sent. Ask your insurance agent to send a certificate to each of these events. You may or may not be charged a small fee for this service if you have them all sent at the same time. Frequently, an event will ask that the certificate be sent with your application. That would be putting the cart before the horse. You can include a note with your application telling the coordinator the name and number of your liability policy, the limits of your coverage, and stating that the certificate will be sent directly from your agent when your application is approved. The coordinators are usually only concerned that your coverage is confirmed before they invite you to their event. The actual certificate needs to be on file prior to the event.

Some Final Thoughts

The whole point of the concession business is to take your product to the customers, rather than, as in the case of a conventional business, to wait for the customers to come to you. In order to justify the time and expense of delivering your product, you must participate in events with the highest potential for profit. And you must customize your selection of events to suit your business. Vendors must consider and weigh an event's sales potential, cost, and logistics to determine whether it's right for them. For example, obviously a large fair with an attendance of hundreds of thousands may seem tempting for its high sales potential. But a single hot dog vendor would only sell as many hotdogs as is physically possible, no matter how many attendees walk through the gate. Conversely, a booth with high operating costs may book an event at which it is the only food booth. But though it may capture every sale, if the attendance is low, the booth would show very little if any profit. Another example: If you are selling cheese doodles, why book an event that you know has already scheduled eight cheese doodle booths? These are just a few examples using sales and cost to illustrate a point. Weighing the logistical factors of an event may be harder. Perhaps you would think twice about an event that starts the day after the previous event ends. A vendor with personal limitations or whose booth has restrictive space requirements or limited maneuverability would need to consider these aspects as well. All vendors have goals and limitations. They must identify what they are and work hard to find the events that are the most profitable and suitable for them. (See Appendix 2 for examples of an Event Information Worksheet and an Event Schedule.)

> Here's a tip: Don't be too quick to write off a poorly performing "first-time event." If other vendors seemed to be doing all right, perhaps you just need to make a few adjustments to your business before trying the event again. As frustrating as it is to be the only booth without customers, it can be turned into a good learning opportunity. Look at it this way: The event provided you with a lot of time to analyze what you could do differently to become more competitive.

Part 4

It's Showtime!

CHAPTER 11

Putting It All Together for Your First Event

By now, you have spent many months researching, planning, and designing your concession business. You have decided on your menu and acquired everything you need: your booth, equipment, signs, and vehicles. You have also dedicated yourself to researching and scheduling some good events, filled out applications, acquired all of the appropriate licenses, and purchased insurance. It's now time to get the show on the road.

Do a Trial Run

If you haven't already thought of it, it is a very good idea to set up your entire operation before you leave home. A dress rehearsal will not only tell you if everything is operating correctly but will also verify whether or not anything has been overlooked. You might consider throwing a booth warming party in your yard. Invite friends and family to sample the food, give feedback, offer suggestions, and, then, wash it all down with a celebratory beer bottle broken against the bow of your booth. After the exercise is complete, you can leisurely practice tearing down and loading everything up in an organized fashion. Your first event will be particularly stressful, and you will be glad you took the time to test drive your operation. It will also be good to know you carefully loaded everything in such a way that you can find anything you need without frantically tearing everything apart.

Stocking Up on Supplies

A day or two before your event, you will need to stock up on supplies. Most vendors have a long list of supplies they buy for each event. Rather than depend on your memory to recall everything you need, make a permanent shopping list of every item that gets used up and either frequently or occasionally needs to be restocked. This complete list will ensure that you never forget anything. It's also a useful tool for taking inventory in preparation for the next event. Make enough copies to last the season.

Sample Shopping List

Fries
___Potatoes
___Fry Oil
___Ketchup
___Salt

Corn Dogs
___Corn Dogs
___Mustard

Beverages
___Bottled Drinks
___Ice

Paper Products
___Trays
___Tissues
___Napkins
___Paper Towels
___Garbage Bags

Cleaning Supplies
___Dish Soap
___Hand Soap
___All Use Soap
___Bar Towels
___Fryer Cleaner
___Bleach

By designing and printing your own shopping list, you will be much less likely to forget something when you are shopping for supplies. This list is an example of what a shopping list for a menu selling curly fries, corn dogs, and bottled and canned beverages might look like.

Any time you do an event for the first time, it is hard to guess how much inventory you will need. If you don't have an extra person available to go for more supplies during the event, the nearest supply store is too far away, or, if you use a product that must be special-ordered, you will need to consider carefully how much stock to bring with you.

Most new vendors make one of two mistakes. Either they think they are going to set the world on fire with sales, or they grossly underestimate what they have gotten into. They either buy far too much stock or too little. If sales are slow, they must pack their entire inventory home again to save for the next event. Even worse, if it's perishable, they must toss it in the trash. Or, if sales are brisk, they might run out of product on Saturday morning one hour after the parade gets out and must scramble to restock for the remainder of the event.

Ideally, your first event will be small. By considering your first trip out a practice session, you can arrive with a modest amount of inventory and focus more of your attention on working out kinks than on the stress of experiencing a loss on your large outlay for stock. By the second trip out, you will have made a few improvements to your operation and have a much better idea both what your concession is capable of and how much stock to bring.

There are several things you can do to help determine how much inventory you need to bring. First, do some rough math. If you know how long it takes to prepare and serve a single serving, you can calculate the maximum number of servings you can possibly serve in an hour. Multiply that by how many hours you will be open for business during the course of the event. You definitely don't need to stock more than what is physically possible to sell. Remember: This is a best-case scenario. Before you get too excited, remind yourself that the kind of luck it takes to do an event that is solidly busy from start to finish is extremely rare. If you could possibly factor in all of the many known and as yet unknown factors that will influence your success, your likely sales scenario would be quite different. In actuality, nearly all events are normally slow but then have a spike in sales during certain times of the day, such as lunch, dinner, when the parade is over, or in the evening, when the main attraction is beginning.

> Here's a tip: It is very common for the sales on Friday to be 1½ times that of Thursday, for Saturday to double Friday, and for Sunday to be similar to Friday.

Second, go back to your business plan where you performed a cost of product analysis. From these previous calculations, you should be very familiar with your product cost and profit margin. Now do some additional rough math. Estimate the total expense of doing the event. By dividing the total event expenses by the profit of an average serving, you can learn how many servings you need to serve before you will show a profit. For example, assume the following:

Event Expenses		Menu	
Space fee	$175	BBQ Sandwich	$4
Health Permit	60	Can of Pop	+1
Vehicle Fuel	90		$5
Propane	20		
Motel Room	100	Average Serving	$5
Staff Wages	400	Profit Margin	x .80
		Profit per Serving	$4
Total	$845		
		Event Expenses	$845
		Profit per Serving	$4
		Servings	211

You now know that you will need to stock at least enough inventory to sell 211 orders to break even. It would not be unreasonable to want a profit that triples your expenses, in which case you should have with you enough inventory to serve 633 orders.

Third, refer again back to your all-important business plan where you planned adequately for storage and freezer capacity. If you use product that is to be kept frozen, you can load up your freezers. Any frozen product that isn't sold will still be good for the following event. Cases of canned or paper products will never spoil, and, if you've got enough room for storage, you can always just have plenty on hand. On the other hand, perishable products, such as fresh fruit and vegetables, will only last for a few days. Pay particular attention to any product you use that needs to be special-ordered or cannot be readily purchased from a regular grocery store.

Ice

If you will be using ice in your beverages or ice chests, you must carefully plan how you will store enough ice to fill your needs. Ice, being what it is, melts quickly. Most fairs and large events understand the importance of ice to food vendors and provide a supply conveniently on-site for the vendors to purchase as needed. Events that are sponsored by Pepsi or Coke will often have ice delivered to the vendors. Check with the coordinators about this in advance. At smaller events, it is the vendor's responsibility to supply his or her own ice. When the weather is hot or beverage sales are brisk, a vendor can go through an astonishing amount of ice in a single day. Therefore, be prepared to either have plenty of freezer space or someone available to run to the nearest store to restock when your ice gets low. Vendors who use a large amount of ice will sometimes invest in an ice machine.

Cash Handling

One of the easiest things to forget on your way out the door to an event is your cash. By always having an adequate supply of one and five dollar bills and coins, if needed, you will never get caught in the middle of a rush without enough change. Many customers come to an event loaded with twenty-dollar bills, which rapidly deplete all of the vendor's supply of ones and fives. If you do get caught short of change, the carnival game joints, ticket booth, or office can usually help you out. It's advisable to bring two hundred dollars in ones and three hundred in fives.

In the course of doing business, you will be handling a lot of cash and must have a system for keeping your money organized and secure. Many vendors prefer to use a cash register for managing their money as well as for the additional benefit of a tape of the day's sales activities. The register can be programmed to track the sale of each item on your menu, making bookkeeping, inventory auditing, and cost analysis very simple. Also, events that charge a percentage of gross sales as a space fee will require that you use a cash register. When a cash register is not required, some vendors mount a cash drawer under the counter. Others may use a cash box. If your booth does not readily provide a secure location for storing or handling cash, you may want to use a bankroll kept in an apron pocket or a fanny pack. Carnival game joints, where the operators actively make change while they're constantly moving, frequently use a bankroll. If done correctly, it is the fastest and safest way to handle large amounts of cash. The technique is to start with a manageable roll of ones and fives. Loosely fold the bills in half with the large denomination bills on the inside. Then put the roll in your pocket. When a customer hands you money, open the roll with your thumb, put any fives or tens on the top, large denomination side, and any ones on the bottom. Put the twenties in a different pocket for safekeeping. If change is required, just peel off the required bills from the top or bottom and then put the roll back into your pocket. If you consistently put the bills on the appropriate side, your money will always be organized. Frequently remove the excess bills so the bankroll remains a manageable size. With a little practice, a bankroll can take bills and give change much more quickly than a register or drawer. This is important. The exchange of money can be an agonizingly slow and cumbersome process. Customers are always slow to pull out wallets or rummage through purses. By using a bankroll, you can stay productive rather than just stand at the register while the transaction is completed. Whatever your cash handling method, it is a good idea to move accumulated cash frequently to a more secure location within your booth during the course of the day. Depending on your situation, the best place may be your own deep pocket.

At the end of the day, most vendors take their bank bag full of the day's earnings into a secure location to sort and face the bills and prepare the starting cash bundles for the fol-

One vendor I know leaves his cash inside a dirty lunch bucket on the floor of his beat-up old pickup truck, where it's deliberately surrounded with old fast food garbage. No one would guess that the lunch bucket holds thousands of dollars. This is not a method for storing cash that I recommend.

lowing day. Over the course of an event, you will accumulate a lot of cash that needs to be stored in a secure location until you can get to a bank. Vendors have safes built into their motor homes, build secret compartments, plant decoys, or even leave it in plain sight.

Don't Forget Miscellaneous Supplies

A concession cannot operate effectively without an assortment of extra tools and supplies. You will always be glad to have with you the following:

- *Hand truck*, for loading and unloading propane bottles, equipment, and cases of supplies.

- *Bungee cords*, for attaching signs and almost anything else that is flapping in the wind.

- *Duct tape*, for a fix-all.

- *Toolbox*, with a good variety of hand tools.

- *7/8" open wrench*, for the propane bottle fittings.

- *A jar full of assorted nuts, bolts, screws, and hose washers.*

- *Potable water hoses*, at least 100', in an assortment of lengths for reaching distant water faucets. If the water is used to fill your water tank, prepare food, or wash dishes, the health department requires the hose be "potable." Otherwise, a regular garden hose will suffice.

- *Electric cords*, 100' of 12-gauge for reaching a distant power source, plus an assortment of lengths and sizes. Some fire marshals expect all cords to be grounded and all power taps to have an internal circuit breaker.

- *Clamp lights* with extra bulbs. The health department requires that all lights used inside a food booth have a protective covering. If the lamp gets broken, bits of glass cannot be allowed to get into the food. Florescent tube lights can be covered with clear acrylic sleeves available at a Cash and Carry wholesale grocer and possibly at hardware stores.

- *Fire extinguisher.* 2A:10BC is the minimum size required. Any booth that cooks will likely be required to carry at least a 40B:C. If you cook with grease, the fire marshal may require an extinguisher as large as one having a "K" rating.

- *Padlocks.*

- *Hose faucet Y.* At nearly all events, several booths will need to tap into a single water faucet. Carry several spares.

- *Vinyl tarps* for rain or sun protection.

- *Ratcheting tie-down straps* for securing heavy objects in transit.

- *Electric generator.* The quieter the better.

- *Lawn chairs* to take a load off when you can. The more comfortable, the better.

- *Cell phone* with a charger.

- *Small stepladder.*

- *Wheel chocks.*

- *Wooden blocks* for leveling and steadying tables, equipment, and booths on uneven ground.

- *Ladder* if you need to get on your roof to mount your signs.

It is also important that you take with you all of your paperwork pertaining to the event, such as the event activity schedule, your contract, temporary restaurant permit, and food handler's card. A small file system or brief case of important documents should be kept in your concession.

No matter how carefully you plan for every conceivable calamity, the unforeseen always seems to happen. Walk yourself through an entire event, trying to imagine all of the worst-case scenarios. Make a contingency plan for anything that might potentially go wrong. In my opinion, one of the worst things that can happen is for a breakdown on the side of the road to occur while you are going home from an event on Sunday night and when everything is closed. It can mean spending the night there until morning, when you can get help. Nor do I enjoy roadside repairs at any time, with semis rocketing past every ten seconds. The following is a short list of potential solutions to common problems:

- Spare tires, parts, and tools for roadside repairs.

- Spare equipment. If you use a piece of equipment that is not easily replaced or repaired and you cannot operate without it, bring a spare.

- Spare parts for equipment in your concession. Examples: heat lamp bulbs, fryer thermo-coupler.

- Possible extra helpers. What would happen if you or a worker became sick or was injured during an event?

- Emergency contact phone numbers.

- A fully-charged cell phone.

Loading up

Before you hit the road, be sure that everything you are hauling is securely fastened to prevent anything from falling over while you travel. I can tell you firsthand that you don't want to arrive at an event to find that everything that was in the refrigerator when you left is now rolling around on the floor—or even worse, that the freezer has fallen over and smashed your counter. Also, by doing a thorough pre-trip inspection of your vehicles, you can save yourself a lot of headaches by catching preventable problems before they happen. It may be helpful to have a checklist of every task you must perform before you lock the door and drive away. No one likes to get twenty miles down the road and then suddenly not be able to recall turning off the kitchen stove.

This truck and trailer are ready to head off to an event. The truck provides living quarters and storage. The trailer holds the concession tent and all of the equipment and stock.

CHAPTER 12

Your Grand Opening

Setting Up at Your First Event

It's important that you arrive at your event well before it opens. Many vendors like to arrive one or two days early when they have plenty of room to maneuver and time to set up before the grounds become crowded with vendors. Your event papers may tell you what time a coordinator will be on-site to assist the vendors. When you arrive, leave your vehicle parked in an area that is out of the way while you locate the coordinator to learn the location of your booth space. Set-up day at most events is chaotic, with vendors trying to get their vehicles into position, their equipment unloaded, and extra vehicles removed from the grounds to allow room for other vendors to get in.

Once you have learned the location of your space, don't feel pressured to rush while setting up your booth. If you are backing a trailer into position, it is better to take as much time as you need to do it right, rather than risk hitting an obstacle or another vendor's booth. You also want to wiggle the trailer as many times as necessary to get it lined up correctly with the other booths. This is important. There are many inconsiderate vendors who like to set their booths up several inches farther into the midway at the expense of the other booths, for the benefit of increased exposure for themselves. Some coordinators literally draw a frontage line over which no part of a booth, awning, sign, trashcan, or anything else can extend. If that is not the case where you are at, line the front corner of your booth with that of your neighbor's. If you as yet have no neighbors, ask the coordinator for the exact perimeter of your space. If you have a trailer with an awning, inquire whether the awning must be behind your frontage line. You want to be clear about this before you unhook your truck and set up your booth. If you have a tent, be sure to set your booth up as close to your frontage line as you rightfully can. I can guarantee that your neighbors will. If a neighboring booth comes in later and sets up over the line, you have every right to request that it be moved back so that your booth is not "buried."

The coordinator can tell you where the electrical and water hookup is, as well as where to park your extra vehicles. If you are like most vendors, once you get settled into your booth space, the stress of preparing for and traveling to the event will subside. You will have a chance to relax while you enjoy setting up and can anticipate a good event.

A pole tent set-up. The poles and canopy have been removed from the truck and roughly assembled like tinker toys.

The signs and canopy are secured to the frame, and the tent is being lifted up on its legs.

The skirts and equipment are installed, and it's ready for customers.

Your Booth Location, Location, Location

The importance of your booth location cannot be overstated. Although this factor is generally in the hands of the coordinator and largely out of your control, the impact that your location has on your business is too profound not to discuss it further. There are occasions when you will need to select a space from several available options. At other times, you may need to negotiate for a different space when your assigned space is unsatisfactory. Understanding the dynamics of pedestrian traffic flow and your space location relative to that flow is critical in either case. Acquiring a sense for what does or does not make a good booth space requires time and the benefit of experiencing many different events. From the moment the coordinator informs you of your spot, stop and take an overview of the event to try to determine if the location will work for you. Will your booth fit? Do your immediate neighbors sell the same menu as you? Are there trees or other obstacles blocking your exposure? And what is the likely flow of pedestrian traffic?

A pole tent next to a custom-built trailer, next to another pole tent in the process of being set up.

Determining the traffic flow at an event that you have never experienced can be a little tricky. Crowds of people generally move like cattle down a highway. People follow each other, are reluctant to go against the flow, stay on the right side of the road, pass on the left, and don't like to walk any farther than they have to. At a large event, such as a fair, notice where the entrance gate is, the main entertainment, the carnival, the restroom, and anything else that may cause an ebb and flow of foot traffic. Be cautious of being placed too near the entrance gate. Most people want to check out their options before they will buy anything. Even if it turns out that they like your menu best, they will rarely backtrack to make a purchase. Likewise, if you are the last booth, the people will already have made a purchase before they get to your booth.

Who Has Seniority?

When doing an event for the first time, don't be surprised if the space you are assigned is less than ideal. Most event coordinators realize that previously attending vendors should be given priority when they are assigning booth spaces. It's a matter of paying your dues, so to speak. If, however, you arrive at an event and learn that your space is so poor that you have no hope of having enough sales to earn a fair profit, you may want to request a different space. It doesn't hurt to ask. If the coordinator refuses to reassign your space, you will have to decide whether it is in your best interest to forfeit the event or stick it out in hopes of recovering some of your costs. Sometimes, with a little delicate diplomacy, a coordinator can be made to realize they really have done you a disservice and will be willing either to find you a different space or to refund your space fee. I say "delicate diplomacy" because at this point in your business you are developing relationships that will greatly influence your business from here forward. The first impression you make should not be as someone whom is difficult to get along with.

Health Department Inspections

Within the first day or two of the event, the County Health Inspector will spend time in your booth to check your licensing status, structural compliance, and proper food handling procedure. Most inspectors are pleasant and eager to assist in your food-handling education. They will point out what changes or corrections need to be made, observe you make any necessary corrections, sign you off, and depart. If you need to make more extensive changes, they will check back with you later to be sure that you have brought your booth into compliance.

Hiring and Managing Your Staff

Nearly every successful concession business is run by the effort of more than one person. Even small pushcart operators have a difficult time manning their booths single-handedly through an entire event from start to finish. A person working alone cannot easily take a break for food, to use the toilet, to get more supplies, or to solve any problems that may crop up during the event. Having a second person available not only relieves the operator of these concerns but also makes the event more enjoyable by allowing the operator time to relax or visit with other vendors. Unfortunately, there are many times when there isn't anyone available to help. At other times, the event may not be big enough to warrant the expense of hiring someone. For many small concessionaires working alone is do-able, albeit exhausting. Once a rhythm is developed of taking orders, collecting money, and dishing out food, a single person can stay abreast and keep the line moving well enough. But, as the day goes on without a letup in sales, you may start running out of product or condiments. You are thirsty and hungry and badly need a restroom break. You start to work slower, and your line of customers is now getting longer. In the back of your panicked brain, you know that the sales you're losing because you can't keep up would have paid for a helper many times over.

The size of the operation determines the appropriate number of workers needed to run the concession efficiently and to its capacity. Also, the number of adequate workers may vary during the course of an event. Although it may only require two people to set up, more workers may be needed to operate the booth effectively while open for business. During the peak hours of operation, the booth may need even more workers to keep the money and food flowing while giving workers an opportunity to take a break during a long, busy day.

Most vendors feel that finding adequate help is the most difficult and frustrating aspect of their businesses. If yours is a family-run concession business, you are the envy of the many vendors who must hire workers from outside. A vendor with "free" relatives is every vendor's dream. A family partnership run with the assistance of pleasant, hard-working youngsters, who are of the opinion that your gratitude is pay enough, is a vendor's nirvana. It's much more likely, however, that your young people will be willing to work in exchange for spending money and to help pay the cost of college tuition. Young people who work in a concession acquire self-confidence, job skills, communication skills, and a work ethic. Although they may not realize it until they acquire the perspective that only punching a time clock can provide, they also have fun.

Finding good helpers can be a challenge. Many vendors hire their kids, their friends' kids, their kids' friends, and their nieces and nephews. High school and college students make excellent employees. They are generally energetic, hard working, and not intimidated by the inconveniences of being "on the road." If you don't already have a supply of possible workers, try advertising at local high schools and colleges.

Here's a tip: A busy fair or festival is not an appropriate place to bring your small children. Too many family-run concessions allow their bored small children to run as wild as renegade circus elephants during the entire event. Not only is this unsafe for the kids, but it is also unfair to neighboring vendors. If your kids are too young to work, get a babysitter.

Working in a food concession is not rocket science. Workers should, however, possess the same desirable character traits of employees in most people-oriented businesses. An honest and reliable worker, who is also clean, friendly, outgoing, and energetic, is ideal. Additionally, because the concession business depends on maximizing sales during peak sales times, a worker must also be able to work quickly and competently while confidently managing hordes of impatient, hungry customers.

A worker who has had previous food service experience will have a much better grasp of the details of safe food handling procedure than will someone who has not. Although most counties only require that one person with a food handlers card be on duty at all times, many vendors require that all of their workers carry a food handlers card. Others may only ask their helpers to read the food handlers handbook.

In most cases, a concession worker will spend much of his or her time being the cashier. This creates frequent opportunities to pocket money on the sly. The best defense you have against theft is to know your business. Although you may never catch the thief in the act, you should always have a pretty good idea how much revenue the booth has produced and a good instinct for inconsistencies. Also, requiring the cashier always to verbalize loudly each order, the price, and amount of change made to the customer, lets you know what has transpired at the cash register even when your back is turned. This procedure also protects the cashier from the customer who makes false accusations that an error was made.

The final thing is to be honest with your workers about your expectations. There are times when you simply cannot oversee the cashier. By initiating an honest, fair-minded, team-oriented policy from the outset, the incentive for dishonesty may be eliminated. In some cases, the only way to know definitively that your workers are honest is to conduct a daily pre-opening/closing inventory audit. If the amount of product used does not jibe with sales receipts, something may be amiss. (See the sample audit form in Appendix 2.)

Your worker hiring policy may include the presentation of a simple document that spells out your expectations of your workers and that also addresses the intangible aspects of your business. An outline of your business principles, policies, and expectations may include the following:

Business Values. While on the job, your workers represent your business identity. In order to present your business to the public, event coordinators, your colleagues, and your customers in the best possible light, workers must first understand your business principles and values. Food concessionaires are still trying to undo the long-held common misconception that food booth operators are dirty and dishonest. By articulating your high standards for cleanliness, product quality, service quality, and appropriate interaction with the public, your workers will be clear where you stand on their role in representing your business.

Hiring Policy. A simple list of your specific expectations and possible reasons for termination will leave no doubt what is expected of them. If you expect your workers to be clean, appropriately dressed, ready for work at a specific time, to wear an apron, to adhere to health department regulations, to refrain from socializing during business hours, to abstain from drinking alcohol or using drugs, to abstain from stealing money from you, to do the work that is required, and so on, you should say so.

Paying Your Help

You may have noticed that in this book workers are not referred to as "employees." For most food concession operators, managing the business end of hiring employees "by the book" is simply unrealistic. Although there are a few who hire employees for the season and do pay compensation insurance, payroll taxes, base and overtime wages, allow required break and lunch periods, and so on, most concessionaires simply don't. The nature of the business makes it logistically too complicated to keep track of the details of an employee's activities for the purposes of filing withholding tax. Most vendors who hire people they know will pay their workers the same way a business would pay a self-employed independent contractor. A deal is struck, the job is performed, and the fee is paid for the service provided. This is additionally true for vendors who hire local help on-site at each event. Paying those helpers any other way would be nearly impossible. For your protection from inquisitive government agencies and more particularly from potential worker lawsuits, you may want to consider having your workers sign a written agreement that provides that the individual is not an employee, but rather is self-employed and is therefore responsible for paying his or her own taxes. In the event of an IRS audit, there is a litmus test the IRS uses to determine the true employee status of a helper. It may want to know the degree of behavioral control the business owner has over the helper, whose tools are used to do the job, whether the worker has any financial risk in the endeavor, and whether the helper's services are available elsewhere. Check with your state and federal agencies to educate yourself about specific business and employer criteria and obligations regarding hiring employees. If you decide to hire "by the book," the paperwork and tax-paying tasks can be done for you by employee management companies. They are well worth their fees.

Depending on your situation or relationship with your helpers, you may want to offer them a choice between payment options: cash for labor or as a regular employee with taxes withheld. If they choose cash, they should also be willing to sign a contract statement. While planning your hiring policy, calculate the cost and benefits of each option before you hire. You may find that it is more beneficial to hire someone as an employer and pay hourly wages and withholding than it is to pay someone in cash. Consider the amount of time you need their help, whether they are living with you on the road, and whether you need the physical help of setting up even though the booth is not yet producing revenue. Also consider whether your employer/employee relationship could influence the attitude and quality of your help.

When doing an event for the first time, it is hard to know how many helpers you will need or whether you will even need them at all. It is hard to pay the workers when an event is disappointingly slow and the cash register is empty. Unfortunately, this is just one of the risks that we all take. In my opinion, it is worth the risk. I am more than happy to pay my workers for their time at slow events because I know that there are far more times that I am eternally grateful they were there to help. Without their help, I would never be able to do any successful events.

Some concessionaires pay their workers an hourly rate. If business is slow, they can let them go. Others pay a flat rate per day or per event. Still others pay a minimal flat rate with a bonus contingency. The bonus may hinge on a commitment to work for the entire season, with the bonus paid at the end of the season. Or the bonus may depend on how hard the worker worked, relative to how busy the booth was. I prefer to pay a guaranteed flat rate whether the day is four hours long or twelve. I then give bonuses on an individual basis, which reflects how busy we were and how grateful I am for their services. No matter how successful the day, if a worker shows up late, takes more than his or her share of breaks, or is hesitant to pitch in, I would not give as large a bonus as I would to someone who is ready and willing to do his or her best job. The bonus awarded for a very busy day also gives the worker a stake in the booth's success.

Here's a tip: By placing a tip jar on the front counter for your workers, they receive instant gratification and motivation for providing your customers with good service.

Good help is good to have.

The crew, hard at work.

CHAPTER 13

Successfully Marketing Your Product

Hands down, the best part of the day is after the booth is closed when you trot off to the camper, crack open your favorite snack, and get down to counting the money...unless sales are poor. Then you can't wait to finish up so you can slink away to scrub the big capital "L" off your forehead in private.

There are hundreds of principles and variations of principles that influence the success of a food booth at any given event. Many are controlled by the coordinator, such as booth location, booth/attendance ratio, duplication of menus, and overall organization and promotion of the event. There are many more that are controlled by the vendor, such as your menu, how well you promote your menu, booth appearance, quality of service and product, efficiency, pricing, and consistently returning to the same event. There are still other principles that are out of everyone's hands, such as the weather and the local economy. It's my opinion that in this business the four most important principles that influence sales are: booth space location, desirability of product, signs, and efficiency. Of those four, three are entirely within your control.

Signs Sell

Have you ever noticed how a carnival, pulsating in bright, flashing, colorful lights makes you feel excited and eager? Have you noticed at the carnival how the "floss wagon," selling cotton candy, popcorn, and candy apples, also brightly lit, makes your mouth water? Maybe it's the enchanting atmosphere of excitement that makes the carnival and its less-than-mediocre food so enticing. You can be sure: The folks at the carnival know what they're doing. I'm not suggesting you wrap your respectable BBQ turkey tail sandwich booth in strobe lights. Rather, I'm trying to make a point: In order to have customers, you first need to get their attention.

One of the most important things you can do to influence your success is advertise your menu with a good sign. There is a popular saying in the concession business that "flash is cash," meaning the booth that most captures the public's attention is the booth that captures the most business. One of the main reasons people go to an event is to eat. As they approach the food court, they are already on a mission and eagerly scanning for available options. If you want a chance to earn their money, it's at that moment that your sign must capture their attention. Yes, it's true, quality, service, value, and other marketing principles play a role, but if your sign doesn't inspire enough interest, your menu won't be considered. This principle is of par-

A concessionaire friend of mine was once frustrated by his inability to compete with the other vendors on the midway. His sign, which was mounted below his service window, was simply too low. So he moved it to above his window where it would be more in the crowd's line of vision as they scanned for food. But his sign was still ineffectively lost in the profusion of booths and signs. Finally, he mounted it at the back of his booth, up high and facing the direction of the crowd, where it was the first and only sign people could see as they approached the food court from the carnival. By the time they were close enough to see the other booths, they had already read his sign and decided what to eat. My friend's sales shot up, and he never again assumed that any sign, placed anywhere, is good enough.

ticular influence at events where booths are arranged in a midway format, essentially facing each other down a double row. This is a cutthroat format that is commonly seen at fairs. Here, not only does the effectiveness of your sign matter but also the overall visual appearance of your booth and operation. The quality and visibility of your signs are so influential to sales that it could be said that almost any menu served from nearly any booth can be effectively marketed providing the concessionaire has the good sense to invest in spectacular signs.

This booth has two signs. The top sign says less about the menu than does the bottom sign.

When designing their signs, many novice vendors are influenced by the franchise signs they see at local malls. Most of these signs don't mention what the shops are selling but instead depend on name recognition for the public to know instantly what's being sold. Food concessionaires aren't franchises and don't have name recognition. A concession sign should focus on promoting the sale of a product rather than waste valuable advertising space displaying the name of the business. The public doesn't care about your business name; they only want to know what they can buy to eat. However, there are exceptions. Sometimes your business name can be used to your advantage. Some concessions are named specifically to promote sales. Take, for example, two booths with the charming business names, "Buns on the Run" and "Two Guys and a Grill." The fun-loving public may be attracted to these booths just for grins. In addition to being fun and memorable, these names hint at what's on the menus as well.

It doesn't take a catchy name to lasso customers. However, it would be helpful to have a sign that distinguishes your booth from the others, particularly if your menu is common. Instead of a sign that reads "hot dogs" in big block letters, why not letter your sign with a distinctive typeface and add a large graphic of a wiener?

Product Quality

"Excuse me. Where did you get that? Is it good?" Word of mouth has a large impact on your business, for better and for worse. From your customers' point of view, attending an event is not cheap, and they want to make the most of it. For most people, getting something to eat is an important part of their event experience. People don't mind paying for their favorite treats provided they don't come away feeling cheated. If your food is particularly great, they will spread the word to their friends. If your food is bad, they will advise everyone within earshot not to buy your food.

How does your food taste? Unless you are selling sugar to yellow jackets, your concession business has an uphill climb if your food tastes bad. This is particularly true if you are serving something unique and your customers make their purchase on faith. If your sales pitch implies that your customers will like the taste of your food, you best not disappoint them. Taste is also important when you are selling something common like hamburgers or hot dogs. Everyone knows how these dishes should taste. No customer will return to your booth for a second purchase if his or her initial purchase was disappointing.

This is also true when it comes to portion size. In order to earn an appropriate profit margin on a dish that is expensive to serve, many vendors choose to serve small portions rather than raise their prices.

From what I have seen, the public never appreciates a small serving unless the price is equally small. If the price is normal, the portion should also be normal, and, if the price is high, the portion should follow suit. Your customers will feel cheated otherwise.

That said, no matter how great your food is, your sales will not always reflect its high quality. If you have faith that your customers will be pleased with their purchase, your confidence will see you through the times that slow sales cause you to question everything about your business. No matter what, you are bound to hear a few complaints: "It's not cooked enough"; "It's cooked too much"; "Your service is too slow"; "The portion is too small"; "It costs too much." Your confidence in the quality of your product will help you confidently manage the malcontents without doubting your expertise.

> There are some menus that are so commonplace they don't get much attention. But concessionaires who make an ordinary dish into one that surpasses all expectation will earn a following of dedicated fans. They can develop a very successful business built on their dish that stands alone for its surprising quality.

Promote Sales with Good Presentation

In some ways, the concession business is show business. The customer is buying into the experience as much as the product, and they like to be wowed. I'm not suggesting you have dancing girls in your booth, but rather that you present your booth and your menu in a way that makes people want to pause for a minute to see what you have to offer them.

The public will take a wide berth around a booth that appears dirty. The impression will be that if the booth is shoddy, so is the food. If the workers are unclean, so is the food. And if no one appears to care about the business or service, it's likely no one cares about the quality of the food either. This impression is usually correct. By presenting your operation with a clean, well-kept booth and staff, you tell the public that you care about your product and their patronage.

If you are selling precooked food, present it for display on the front counter behind a sneeze guard so your customers can see how good it looks. If you cook to order, do it with flare. If you have a gift for gab, use it to engage your customers. Anything that gets the public's attention, in a good way, is good for business. What's more, even as your food is walking around the event grounds in the hands of your customers, you want it to continue to make sales for you. Serve your food in a way that is pleasing to the eye. For example, strawberry

I recently met a gal running a little converted RV trailer with poster board signs. Her start-up concession had a fry daddy on a table out back where she prepared her deep fried fruit dessert dish. On the first day, when sales were slow, she walked around the event grounds with samples on toothpicks. As she came by my booth, she said because her menu was different she had managed to get contracts into two of the most coveted events in this area. She was concerned about not knowing if the events would work out for her. Her dish was simple, different but recognizable, affordable and very tasty. Before long everyone was talking, "Have you tried the food at that little booth in the corner? WOW, you have to try it!" By Friday evening, she had a line at her booth that stretched the length of the park. Her line didn't let up for the entire event. Of course, her poor little fry daddy couldn't keep up with her business. Later, when the event had ended, she told me she planned to invest in a big deep fryer and better signs in preparation for the two big contracts she had coming up. Her exhausted grin was as large as her overstuffed bank bag.

shortcake tastes the same with or without a swirl of whipped cream and a strawberry on top. However, without the swirl and strawberry it will not advertise itself. If your food can inspire someone to ask the question, "Excuse me. Where did you get that?" you have done your job right.

It's a challenge to design the front of a booth so that it attracts business. And yet, there are a million ways to do it. Boldly announcing your business with a display using color, shape, height, and depth will influence its sales appeal. For example, imagine in one concession a service table at the front with a cash register and a box of napkins. At the rear of the concession is the food production area. In the concession next door, the front counter has a cash register and napkins, but it also has a four-foot sneeze guard protecting several pans of bright steaming food. Next to the food is a tall beverage dispenser, a condiment bar, and a smiling concessionaire in a bright apron dishing out food and collecting money.

A pop-up tent with a stock trailer. The service counter is made of two wooden cabinets on wheels. This booth has signs hung high, signs hung low, and signs hung down the sides. The colorful product is on display on the front counter.

One of the reasons carnival floss wagons do so well is because they take advantage of the design elements: depth, color, and height. The colorful, easy-to-read signs are frequently back-lit marquees on the window awnings, which wrap around the booth for added exposure and visual depth. Wrap-around signs are also mounted inset on the roof. Carnival floss wagons, unlike independent concessionaires, can even compete successfully for attention with the flashing carnival rides and games joints.

A manufactured "floss wagon" at a carnival. Notice the wrap-around signs and windows. Also, the windows are large and tall, all the better to create a display with hanging cotton candy and licorice ropes.

Provide Quality Customer Service

Providing a quality buying experience for the customer is critical for promoting repeat sales. By offering friendly, helpful, and professional service, you will send your customers away feeling good about selecting your booth over the others. Over the course of a season, you will serve thousands of people but will likely only remember a handful of your customers. However, nearly every customer that bought your food will remember you. Both an exemplary and a less-than-positive buying experience will be remembered. A concessionaire who has a winning personality and provides quality service at the window will nearly always outsell the competition. And developing a good rapport with your customers pays dividends over time. It feels very good to be welcomed back to a community by your steady customers. As the season tiredly wears on, however, keeping a pleasant demeanor gets harder and harder to do.

Here's a tip: People respond to visual stimulation. Further, the better they see something, the better they respond. For example: An ice chest full of beverages on ice will sell far better with the lid open than closed, and a large photograph on a menu board will influence sales better than a written description. Visibility promotes sales.

Friendly service.

Any time you are serving large numbers of people, conflicts are sure to arise. It can be difficult to know how to deal with difficult customers. My view is: The customer is sometimes right. Even when you know for certain that the customer is wrong, is it really worth the time, energy, and possibly bad PR to convince them of that? On the other hand, if you are the target of a scam, verbal abuse, disrespect, or property abuse, you will probably want to stand your ground.

Setting Prices

For your concession business to be successful, your selling price must, at the very least, include the cost of your product, your overhead cost, and a profit margin. Like any

> I have on more than one occasion backed down to a malicious customer, allowing him or her to save face and potentially saving myself from being the victim of vindictive after-hours retaliation with a can of spray paint. I have also, on many more occasions, called to task both kids and adults when they were disrespectful or their bad behavior affected my business or personal property.

business, vendors also use price as a competitive strategy. Some set their prices lower than everyone else to increase their market share. Others have flexible pricing where they change their prices according to customer demand, what other vendors are charging, what the market will bear, or what their overhead costs are at a particular event. Some just set their prices at the normally accepted price and stick to it. If you sell something that is unique or particularly special, you can also set the price high to convey prestige.

Whatever your pricing strategy, you should first do a cost analysis to determine your product and overhead costs. (See Chapter 4, Product Cost Analysis.) Finding the correct price for your product is critical to showing a profit margin that's large enough to stay in business. With all the quick cash being made, it is easy to believe the business is healthy and viable, when it isn't. By keeping a careful eye on the profit and loss statements, the product cost analysis, and your selling price, a concession business can stay afloat long-term, even though it only pays its way for a fraction of a year. Your pricing may need to be adjusted periodically because your business expenses will change over time. Most new vendors have a difficult time with pricing. It usually goes something like this:

- Most nonprofits set their prices too low. Nonprofits don't need to "stay in business." They only need to earn more than their overhead, which is usually lower than normal due to donated labor, (sometimes) donated product, and lower licensing costs.

> Here's a tip: At some events, new vendors can establish themselves very quickly by setting their prices low to entice buyers to try their product. Once they have established a following, they raise their prices for a better margin of profit.

- New concessionaires who sell an unusual menu often set their prices too high. This might be a good approach if they don't plan to stay in business. If you plan to stay in business, however, your business needs repeat customers. In some economies, high-priced food is hard to sell, no matter how good it tastes or correctly portioned it is. In other areas, some people are willing to shell out good cash for a decent meal, but they do so on the assumption that they will get their money's worth.

- New concessionaires who sell regular fair food frequently set their prices too low. They are up against stiff competition and don't have enough confidence to compete head-to-head with the more experienced vendors. They may be right. However, by selling low, if they stay in business at all, they will never make enough money to invest back into the business. They will not be able to afford a better booth and better signs so they can compete more effectively with the senior vendors. They are in a difficult catch-22. In this case, I suggest they put something unique on their menu. Keep the standard fair food, but also add something that can have its own niche in the midway market. Then, charge a healthy price for it.

When weighing the pros and cons of your pricing philosophy, keep in mind the big picture. If your prices are low, you will sell more food. But you will also use more stock and work harder. Because of this, you will also need more helpers, spend more time stocking up and prepping, carry more stock weight, and consume more propane. If your prices are high, you will sell less but make more money on each sale. You will work less, need fewer helpers, consume less propane, and need less time to stock up and prep. Setting your prices high might be considered a good approach, unless your prices are too high, in which case, you will not have enough customers to buy gas for the trip home.

Here's a tip: Whenever possible, many vendors prefer to round their prices up to the nearest dollar. The time and energy saved by eliminating the time and energy it requires to make change, is profit gained.

Many states with a state sales tax require the price of a dish be posted, including the tax added. Most vendors round the price up to the nearest dollar and pay the tax themselves rather than charge the customer. However, if you are doing an event that charges a percentage of gross sales for the space fee, you may want to bring a lot of change and charge extra for tax. The tax is subtracted from your gross sales before the space fee is calculated. You can still try to round up so that the price including the tax totals an even dollar, but you need to post the numbers on your menu board so the public is fully informed. Your sign might look like this:

> **Meat Ball Sandwich**
>
> **$6.00 tax included**
>
> ($5.58 + .42 tax)

It must be noted that some events, particularly fairs, like to initiate a price-control policy. They frequently set a minimum price that vendors can charge for certain items. This policy prevents the vendors from having price wars. It also prevents nonprofits, who have lower overhead, from under-pricing the professional vendors. Occasionally, events also set maximum prices with the idea of keeping their event affordable for fair goers. This policy is unfair to the vendors, as well as unnecessary. Event coordinators have no knowledge of each vendor's overhead or product cost and should leave price control to the market.

Efficiency for Maximizing Sales

"NO SOUP FOR YOU!" is a sign I would like to wear on my forehead during a rush. Anyone familiar with the TV episode of *Seinfeld* in which Jerry, Elaine, George, Kramer, and Norman are trying to buy soup from the "Soup Nazi," a soup vendor who acts like a dictator, will know what I'm talking about when I say that during a rush we wish our customers would either snap to or get out of the way. That would take care of the slow customers outside your booth, but what about efficiency inside your booth?

After successfully applying every marketing principle to your business, you will still not be successful unless you have your act together in the booth. In order to maximize sales during a rush, your business must run with the rapid efficiency of a shark in a fish bowl. Every aspect of your food preparation and service, from booth style, equipment capacity, equipment layout, to quality and quantity of workers, must be implemented in a way that allows for maximum productivity. If you hope to serve hundreds of servings of food a day, every piece of equipment must be large enough and have the heating or cooling capacity to do the job efficiently. The layout of your equipment and workspace within your booth must be such that each worker can perform their tasks with the least amount of steps, effort, and time. And your workers must be trained and able to work quickly and competently.

As strange as it may seem, maximum sales during a given period of time will be achieved when you have a line of customers waiting to order. It is with this line that your front counter workers must stretch themselves to get as many orders as they can, as quickly as they can, and your back counter people must perform at optimal efficiency. The rush is on, and your entire operation must operate at peak capacity. If your menu is one that requires your customers to wait while their food is prepared, encourage them to form two lines, one for ordering and another for pickup. People don't mind standing in line as long as they can see that the workers are working fast and efficiently and the line is moving. On the other hand, if your workers appear to be half asleep or incompetent, your would-be customers will be quick to find a different booth to buy from. Customers are always impatient to tell you what they want. Once they have done so, however, they will happily wait while you prepare their orders. It's a good idea to collect their money at the time they place their orders. The monetary commitment ensures they won't change their minds and walk off.

> Here's a tip: When business is slow, it's easy to get comfortable in the fresh air behind the booth. As tempting as it is, it will cost you sales. Your presence inside your booth ready to serve encourages business, particularly if you get peoples' attention with a smile, a friendly comment, or a sales pitch. When you're preoccupied with your nose in a book or playing games on your cell phone, the folks who are interested in your menu may not want to disturb you.

In fact, a fast moving line in front of your booth helps promote business. First, the line implies that your food is good enough to wait for. More than that, however, your line is your audience, and this is your time to shine. Nearly every set of eyes in the line will be on your operation. This is your chance to engage your customers with your efficiency, the quality of your service, your proficiency at food preparation, your engaging conversation, and, finally, your wonderful product as another smiling customer carts away a serving of your world's greatest BBQ snail tails. People walking by see your product and step into line. That's how it's done.

One small elephant ear booth, one long line.

The Benefits of Repeated Events

Participating in the same event for repeated and consecutive years has many benefits. Once you've done an event, you can keep doing it for as long as you want, unless you do something to anger the coordinators, in which case, you will not be invited back. Or, in some cases, drastically changing your menu will be enough to cause you to lose your spot. The benefits of continuously supporting an event are compounded each year.

Seniority. Building a good working relationship over time with the coordinators gives the vendor a lot more clout in the form of seniority. Although some coordinators don't recognize the value of a vendor repeatedly supporting their event, most do and are willing to give senior vendors preferential treatment in the form of choice of location and top billing when limiting duplication of menus. Seniority also provides an opportunity to develop what's known as "your spot." By being permitted to set up in the same location year after year, your customers will always know where to find you. Oddly, if your location gets moved, even just to across the midway, for many of your repeat customers, the spell will be broken.

Simplicity. Each consecutive visit becomes easier. You will know all of the particulars of the event, including how much stock to bring and when to be geared up for a busy period. Many first-year vendors get blindsided by a busy period. They have been sitting around all day without much business, then, when the crowd hits unexpectedly, they are not prepared with enough product or helpers. Every event has its own idiosyncrasies. Knowing when to arrive extra early, when to bring an extra water hose for a particularly distant faucet, or when to bring hiking shoes to get to the motor home, which must be parked ten blocks away, are just a few of the things that can make an event go much, much more smoothly.

> Here's a tip: Unless your charisma is phenomenal, no coordinator or customer is ever selecting you personally; it's always what's on your menu that interests them.

Increased Sales. Most of all, each year your sales will go up. If your product is good and all things are equal to a previous year, your repeat customers, plus some new customers, will boost your sales. Every event has a large number of people who ritually attend every year. Those people are often a little afraid to spend their money at an unfamiliar and unproven booth. The second time you participate, you will no longer be unfamiliar. After a few years, you will even become a fixture, and your repeat customers will consider buying from you an important part of their event ritual.

Competing on the Midway

Ideally, an event will have the right number of booths and mix of menus to satisfy the needs of the people who attend. Both the public and vendors alike prefer an event with a nice selection of meals, desserts, and snacks from which to choose. The vendors additionally expect that an event will not have too many booths or duplication of menus so there will be enough business to go around. It's the coordinator's job to achieve the right balance. At a well-balanced event, the effect of direct competition on your sales will be insignificant; both you and your competitor will operate at full capacity. Unfortunately, this is frequently not the case. Some vendors usually have an advantage over the others. Maybe they have a better location, have been attending the event longer, or have lowered their prices. Sometimes they may just have a more attractive booth with more effective signage. It is your job to do everything you can to even the score and gain the edge. Very often vendors will develop a false sense of their own ability to make sales. They amble around doing very well at small events with little competition. It's not until they try to compete at a large event that they realize that their booth doesn't measure up to the competition. That's the time to reevaluate your booth, signs, and marketing principles.

As stated earlier, you will only succeed in the concession business if your customers make the decision to stand in your line. There are two main components that influence the creation of a line, the desirability of your product and critical mass. We addressed desirability in Chapter 4, Planning the Best Menu for High Profit. Critical mass, however, is determined by attendance, space location, and competitiveness. Unlike attendance and space location, competitiveness can be largely controlled. Nearly all food booths will have some customers during the event. It's your job to make sure that your booth influences more people to make the decision to buy your food instead of your competitor's food. Every customer who buys from your competition is a sale lost. Customers usually make a conscious decision what to buy and from which booth. Though a few may make a purchase spontaneously, your goal is to influence the attendees to make a deliberate decision to schedule their time and spend their money at your booth, not the other guy's booth. How do you do that? Aside from offering a desirable product, you must:

- Get their attention with attractive, easy-to-read signs.

- Draw them in with a clean, attractive booth.

- Prompt their decision with a convincing menu board.

- Make it easy for them to order with a service window or counter that is easily accessible.

- Make them happy with good customer service.

- Satisfy them with efficient, fast-moving service.

- Impress them with an attractive product.

- Please them with correct pricing/portion size.

- WOW them with great tasting food.

Your financial bottom line is determined by the size of the line, how quickly it gets processed, and what margin of profit it produces. Of course, that wonderful line of customers must occur event after event, year after year for you to stay in business.

A high-volume pole tent booth. Notice the bright, graphic, easy-to-read signs lashed inside PVC pole frames. Sneeze guards and beverage tanks across the front counter create a pleasing visual display.

Learn everything you can about how to improve your business by observing your competitors. Be realistic in deciphering which techniques are applicable to your business and which are not. If your competitor has a staff of five, he or she likely has a wider range of options than do you and your staff of two. Once you have made all the mental notes you can, preserve the health of your self-esteem by resisting the constant comparison of your sales to those of your neighbors. The only booth you actually need to beat is your own. This is easier said than done. When doing an event for the first time, you have no benchmark to compare sales with and can only hope to be satisfied with your earnings. The following year you will aim your sights on sales that are at least as high as they were for you the prior year. If they are, you're doing something right.

Unethical Marketing

The food concession business is extremely competitive. In order to be successful, you must do everything you can to encourage the public to buy from you rather than your competitor. That doesn't mean you should practice unfair and unethical marketing activities. You will only succeed in angering your would-be vendor friends. You will not only anger your neighbors at that particular event, but also the word will spread more rapidly than spilled cooking oil, and you will quickly earn a reputation for being a cutthroat. Vendors love to gossip, and any reputation you have will greet you at every event you go to. Some common bad behaviors and unfair sales tactics are:

- *Hawking*. Vendors who call out to the public are disruptive. Whether by offering samples or jokes, they draw the attention of customers away from other booths, to redirect the public's focus on their own booth.

- *Spreading out*. Some vendors like to take up more room than they paid for by placing sandwich boards, extra supplies, equipment, lawn chairs, unruly workers, or other things on the space of their neighbors. Vendors who spread their clutter and unruliness have a negative impact on their neighbors, as well as on themselves.

- *Extending over the line*. Vendors who set up their booths so that they extend farther into the midway than other booths create better exposure for themselves and impede the exposure of their neighbors.

- *Menu expansion.* Some vendors either do not list their entire menu on their applications or add additional menu items after they have observed the menus of the other vendors at an event. This practice undermines any effort that may have been made by the coordinator to control duplicating menus.

- *Stealing ideas.* All vendors borrow ideas from each other. That's how we learn the business. However, there is a big difference between borrowing and stealing. All vendors become angry when another vendor rummages through their trash after dark to look for discarded containers that reveal the ingredients of their prized secret sauce. Any time you take, without asking, another vendor's ideas, make them your own, then use those ideas to take away sales, you are considered to be a thief.

The extent to which a coordinator is willing to police the actions of the vendors varies from event to event. Whereas some prefer to leave the vendors to a free-for-all of doing what they will, others are quick to oversee and enforce a long list of vendor rules. Most coordinators fall somewhere in-between. If you have the misfortune of being neighbors with one of these misfits, you have several options. First, you could choose to live with it. Although we all wish our neighbors would be pleasant company for the duration of the event, some neighbors are simply annoying. If they aren't adversely impacting your business, you might

> Vendors prefer events where the coordinators state their policy and indicate the ground rules. This implies, though sometimes falsely, that the coordinators are aware of these types of problems and plan to stay on top of things.

just want to tolerate them. Second, you could speak to the offender. Sometimes people are offensive without realizing it. Once you pleasantly request them to correct their bad behavior, they are happy to do so. As a last resort, you can complain to the coordinator or fair manager. Most event coordinators are stressed-out from the constant demands of the vendors. If the neighbor's offense is truly a detriment to your business, a diplomatic discussion with the coordinator may be in order. Most fairs and large festivals require that the vendors sign a contract binding them to certain stated rules and obligations. This contract empowers the fair manager to take whatever action he or she deems is appropriate. My advice: Analyze the effect of the offense on your business and sanity, and choose your battles wisely.

Operations and Managing Your Business

Concessionaires lead double lives. The public sees the booth on-site at an event, clean and shiny with the service window open, all of the food prepared, hot and steaming behind the sneeze guard. They see us in our booth cooking, taking orders, refilling the condiment bar, and directing the staff. They see the signs hung where they can read them and the beverages cold with ice. What they don't see is the time and effort it took to make it all so.

What makes it so are the thousands of hours spent managing the business. I'll describe some of these activities in the first person because they are taken out of my personal playbook. As with all concessionaires, your playbook will look a little different. I hope that by understanding my situation and how if affects the way my business is managed, you will be able to make plans for the best situation for your business.

In my case, and for most of us, the season begins in early spring. As early as late February, I make the call to the state department of tourism for the new edition of the state event calendar. While waiting for that to arrive, I look at my last season's event schedule and sales ledger. It's time to start considering which events I will return to and which I will try to replace. Many festivals are scheduled always to land on the first, second, third, or fourth full weekend of the month. However, county fairs seem to change dates frequently. I can get a jump on learning the dates of all the county fairs in the state by visiting the state fair association's website. While there, I also look at the date of the fairs I would like to do but have not yet done. Then, in my newly purchased monthly pocket calendar (with the big squares for each date), I mark in ink the events I go to every year. Once that is done, I can see which weeks are still blank. When the new state event booklet (or any other event listing guide) arrives, I go through it and highlight any events that look like interesting candidates for the dates I need to fill. These events are marked in my calendar in pencil. I also keep a list in a pocket notebook of these "possible" events that I need to contact with the name of the coordinator, the phone number, and the event website, if there is one. If the event does have a website, I visit it before I call the coordinator on the phone. It's nice to have as much information as possible upfront, so I can use the phone conversation to fill in the gaps.

With event scheduling underway, I now make a list of all the other early season activities. Most of these activities take several weeks or months to complete. These activities may include:

- Updating my promotional pamphlet so it will be ready to send out with applications.

- Filling out and returning event applications as they arrive. Notes are kept on the dates and status of each part of these activities, including the date and amount of fees paid, balances owed, space footage purchased, menu to be served, insurance certificates needed, and any due dates. When events are confirmed, they get marked in the calendar in ink. Follow-up calls are made to coordinators who are slow to respond.

- Making a list of the county of each of my events and calling each county health department for a temporary restaurant permit application. I fill out the early season applications and hold onto the later season ones until I have more capital. By calling for each application in advance, I have the applications in my office and can easily mail them about a month before the event.

- Checking the expiration date on my food handler's cards and renewing them if needed.

- Planning my menu. This activity goes hand-in-hand with scheduling events. Some seasons I sell the same menu all summer whereas other seasons the menu gets changed weekly. I need to know which menu I am applying with at which events.

- Considering my hiring activities. This goes hand-in-hand with scheduling events and menu planning. Before anyone is hired, I need to know how many people I need and when I need them. I give a heads-up to those people who might work to let them know that the schedule is developing and ask whether they are interested in being part of the team this summer. If my usual staff is unavailable, I make plans to post ads at the local colleges. For those who are interested in working, I send a schedule of our events and let the workers pick the dates they want to work. (See the example event schedule in Appendix 2.)

- Starting a list of repairs needed on the trucks, trailers, booth and equipment. At the end of the previous summer, I will have made a list of these tasks because I don't trust my memory through the winter.

- When spring weather improves, bringing out all of the equipment from storage to be thoroughly cleaned and repaired. Of course, the living compartment in the truck is also cleaned.

- Taking care of household chores. Because I am away at events most of the summer, all the yard work and garden activities need to be done as well as possible to minimize the amount of yard work needed during the summer. My hair gets trimmed, and my prescriptions are filled. I try to attend to everything I can now, so I won't be distracted with extra chores once the season starts.

Once the season gets underway, the list of tasks changes. Most of my early events are three days long, Friday through Sunday. I always arrive at the event at least one day in advance, so I have enough room to get my equipment in and enough time to set up. Although I don't usually leave for an event until Thursday, my job begins on Monday. My weekly routine looks something like this:

- Monday: In the morning after returning from an event, my first and favorite job of the week is to pick my dog up from the kennel. After lots of wet dog kisses, I then bring in dirty clothes and left-over food from the truck. While the clothes are being washed, I count and organize the cash (another favorite job), get the bank deposit ready, and make entries in the ledgers. I then make a trip to the bank and grab a few groceries for the few days I'm eating at home. In the afternoon, the truck and trailer are emptied and cleaned.

- Tuesday: Today is the one day during the week I take care of odd jobs like equipment repairs, bill paying, and yard work.

- Wednesday: Today I load up on supplies. It takes several trips to get propane, stock, and groceries for eating while at the event.

- Thursday: Today I leave for the event. After taking the dog to the kennel, I load the ice chests with frozen product, refrigerator items, and groceries. A bag of clothes is packed. All of the ice chests, stock, paperwork, and personal items are loaded into the trailer and truck for the trip. After traveling to the event, I park the trailer and truck and begin the five hour job of setting up.

- Friday: Opening day. In the morning, the staff arrives, and we finish setting up and prepping. The booth is open for business. At the end of the day we clean up the day's mess and prepare the booth for the following day.

- Saturday: In the morning, we rush to get everything ready and open on time. My menu requires my food prep be done in the morning. Once the parade gets out, the booth will be swamped all day. Saturdays are usually stressful. This is the big day, and everything must run perfectly.

- Sunday: The morning is not so hectic. We again prep and prepare to open for the day. During the day, while the staff holds down the fort, I take an inventory of stock and start a list of repairs and tasks for the week ahead. About an hour before closing, we slowly start to wash and put away what we can. At closing, it's time for high-gear cleaning and packing up. I hope to pack up quickly and bring the truck onto the grounds as soon as possible. Some events are very crowded, with vendors bringing in trucks and pulling out trailers. Sometimes, it is so congested with traffic that we must wait several hours for an opening to bring in the truck, get hooked up, and then get off the grounds for the trip home.

As the season progresses, the events become longer. When events are four and five days long instead of only three, the weekly schedule of preparing for the event is condensed into a single day. In planning the management of your own concession business, compare my situation to yours.

- I limit the booth's dimensions. Because I work some events or certain days at some events entirely alone, the booth cannot be any larger than what I can manage. However, the booth is also big enough to make good on a good, strong event with several people working.

- I am not a large person. Without a partner for lifting and carrying, I try to keep the amount of heavy stock and equipment to a minimum. I require my stock trailer to be behind my booth at every event because I cannot unload and reload full freezers and dozens of heavy cases of product and propane tanks.

- I can only be at one place at a time. This is another reason I keep the stock trailer with the booth. Without a second person, I cannot leave the booth to sprint off to the parking lot to retrieve a needed item.

The moral of this illustration is to demonstrate how your personal situation will dictate and control your concession opportunities. Two energetic people without personal limitations or one energetic person who is not opposed to hiring (and depending on) additional staff members may be unlimited in the type or size of concession business they can operate. They can reach for every possible opportunity without regard to logistical limitations. The chores are shared, and they can divide and conquer the events.

In case you question the validity of the concession business, this illustration must also demonstrate to you that if one small, middle-aged woman can make an adequate yearly income from a modest concession business, then the concession business certainly must present a viable opportunity for nearly anyone to make money.

The rush is on.

A custom-built trailer with hungry customers.

CHAPTER 14

Record Keeping

No one likes to keep records, particularly during the chaos of the busy concession season. As a consequence, many vendors either don't bother or keep records that are inadequate. There are many very good reasons to keep track of the financial aspects of the business, as well as to keep a detailed record of your events.

- *For business performance analysis.* You want to know how your business is performing on a monthly and yearly basis.

- *For event performance analysis.* You need to keep a record of your financial activities at each event on which to base future booking decisions.

- *For tax liability purposes.* Accurate records are essential for filing taxes and for substantiating your numbers in the event of an audit.

- *For budgeting and planning.* Good records enable you to forecast your financial needs, make plans to meet those needs, and budget for adequate and timely resources.

- *For calculating costs and setting prices.* Without records, it would be difficult to track the cost of your product in order to calculate prices.

- *For planning and forecasting future events.* You need to have a record of the details of each event for future reference. Take note of how much inventory was used, factors that influenced sales, basic expenses, set-up time, and logistical oddities. Also, take note of who helped, when they helped, and how much they were paid. These details are critical for planning for the same event the following year.

Record keeping is neither hard nor time consuming. By starting with some simple practices, your life as a business owner will be easier. Your knowledge of and enjoyment in the business will be greater, and you will stay on top of your finances and therefore be wealthier.

Bank Accounts

Most business classes advise that when starting a business one of the first and most important things you should do is open a separate checking account for your business. This is particularly true if you share a checking account with someone other than your spouse who is not involved in your business. Good record keeping starts by keeping business expenses and deposits separate from personal ones. It is also requisite for getting through a tax audit unscathed. If you do nothing else to keep records, at least a checking account ledger will provide you with some record of your financial activities. Put simply, if your business checking account runs out of money, you can easily tell that your expenses exceed your income.

Based on their popularity, plastic credit cards seem to be the best thing since the invention of the Tilt O'Whirl. I don't agree but concede they are faster than writing a check. If you like to use plastic, use a separate one for your business. It doesn't need to have your business name on it. One big advantage to using a separate credit card is that it's easier than trying to sort out personal from business expenditures for entry into a ledger. And unlike interest on personal expenses, business expense interest is deductible on your taxes. Having a separate card for your business makes it easy to take advantage of this deduction as well.

Get Organized

Get a file cabinet, boxes for hanging folders, a coffee can, or a large clasp envelope. It's important to save all your receipts, invoices, event applications, licenses, insurance certificates, phone contacts, initial plans, and resources (such as equipment dealers). Some business activities don't provide paper to file. As is the case with post-event information, you have to record the information yourself, perhaps in a small notebook. Make a habit of filing all paperwork pertaining to your business in a way that makes sense to you. Ledgers with a variety of column widths can be purchased from an office supply store and then customized to suit your specific needs. Now that you have it all organized, it is important to organize it further so the numbers will be useful. Many vendors use handwritten ledgers to keep their expenses organized. Some also utilize bookkeeping software, such as Microsoft Money or Quicken, on their computers. Whatever system you are most comfortable with and works best for you should be the one you use.

I find it enjoyable to spend a short time once a month going through my checkbook ledger, jar of receipts, and post-event notebook transferring the numbers into a categorized profit and loss ledger. These monthly exercises are concluded by tallying the month's total income and expenses. I then add an additional column labeled "to date." This column gives a running total through the season of exactly how much I've spent so far in each category. It also tells me when my net income changes from a negative number to a positive one. That usually happens in early July and always inspires a happy sigh of relief. From that point on, it's a race through the season to stuff as much money as possible into my savings account before the season runs out. This is easier said than done. During the same time period, money must be kept in the business checking account to keep the show on the road. And money must also be funneled into the personal checking account to keep the household bills paid. Additionally, any large bills, such as property taxes or medical bills that have been put off must also be taken care of. With good bookkeeping, I know where I stand and can make adjustments to control costs or schedule extra events, if needed to reach my goals.

Tax Filing

Vehicle and traveling costs are a large part of a concessionaire's budget. For tax purposes, be sure to save receipts and track the mileage on vehicles that are used in your business. On the subject of income taxes, I recommend that you educate yourself about tax filing as a small business. No matter how you may feel about paying taxes or plan to address your tax liability, it is a matter that should not be approached with ignorance. Self-employment offers many tax filing angles and advantages that are otherwise unavailable to you. Depending on your situation, you may want to hire a professional tax preparer or accountant. Aside from the value of this person's expertise, it is also nice to have a professional on your side in the event of an audit. One reason many people go into the concession business is because it's a cash business, leaving little paper trail to audit. As some folks say, "The IRS can't put an agent in front of every wienie wagon." On the other hand, if you are like most people, you have an innate dread of hearing personally from the IRS. Furthermore, if you plan to seek financing, tax returns are the only way the self-employed can prove their income to a lender. (See Appendix 2 for examples of an Event Income Statement, a Monthly Expense Log, an Inventory Audit, a Yearly Event Comparison Log, and a Profit and Loss Statement.)

A stock trailer with fold-out rear doors parked behind a double pop-up tent. The concession is closed. Instead of sidewalls, the counters have been covered with tarps.

CHAPTER 15

Finale

If it's Sunday evening, it must be time to close your booth and start tearing down. By now, you are tired of the event and ready to hit the road for home. Most events don't want vendors tearing down any earlier than a specific time. It's dangerous to bring trucks and vehicles onto the events grounds while there are still event goers wandering around. It's also not considerate to the event and other vendors who are still open. When a booth is torn down prematurely, the remaining event goers soon depart, effectively putting an end to the event.

If you have a concession trailer, the job of tearing down is not that difficult. Most vendors like to clean and secure everything inside the trailer, grab miscellaneous items left around, hitch the trailer to the truck, perform a pre-trip inspection, and then off they go. They can quickly leave the event grounds, but once at home they find they have brought the event dirt with them. It's at home that most trailer operators unload their concession trailer to do a thorough cleaning. They then reload in preparation for the next event.

Tearing down a tent or stick joint is another matter. Everything must be cleaned, equipment must be loaded, tent and signs are taken apart, and hoses and cords must be rolled. Finally, everything must be loaded. If it's cleaned, loaded, and organized in just the right way, it won't need to be handled again until you get to the next event.

Do a final pre-trip inspection to be certain you have all of your stuff and that it is all loaded securely. Also, check that the trailer is hitched correctly, that your running lights still work, and that there is still air in your tires. It's not uncommon for a vendor to find that his or her vehicle has been tampered with while it was parked away from the booth. Finally, be sure to leave your space clean. A space that is left inconsiderately dirty will be the last thing the coordinator has to remember you by. If you feel that the coordinator has done a good job, it doesn't hurt to tell him or her so. Then, have a safe trip home.

If you are like me, on the drive home you'll be reviewing the last few days in your head. Smiling into the windshield at the amusing incidents, the new friends you made, and how pleased you were with the quality of your helpers and the way you handled a stressful situation. You will also smile in anticipation of what might be your favorite part of the event—toting a fat bank bag to the bank. You'll also start planning your tasks for the week ahead.

So there you have it. That's the concession business as I see it. Your experiences will be very different from mine, and over time you will likely draw different conclusions. At least with these guidelines to get you started, you will start your business with less debt and perhaps experience some successful events early enough to keep you in business. I have always considered it a shame when someone striving for a modest opportunity to be self-employed can't quite succeed for lack of guidance early on.

The only way to learn this business is to jump in and do it. Your first event will be the hardest. Don't get discouraged. In fact, don't get discouraged by any single event. It takes a season to make the business, and the season is not over until your event calendar has been fulfilled. Even experienced vendors make devastating decisions and experience horrid events. Learn from the bad ones, put them behind you, and prepare for a fresh opportunity at the next event.

EPILOGUE

This concessionaire cannot end without saying a few words about one of the very best aspects of the business, other vendors. We vendors are typically a free-spirited and independent bunch. It's our independence that makes our friendship with each other unique by comparison with all other relationships. During the season, we happily spend much of our time sitting behind each other's booths swapping stories. We gossip and gripe about different events, coordinators, health inspectors, our customers, and other vendors. We all have and understand each other's problems and share the same trials. Our business is unique, and we understand each other in a way no one outside the business can. We are happy to see each other once or twice a year, for at the end of the season, we head off down the highway one last time to lead our other lives.

Although we are competitors, most vendors will do nearly anything to help a fellow vendor. We share knowledge, tools, and a helping hand. Regularly, we will offer to pick up supplies for our neighbors just to save them a trip. The business has its faults, but most of us wouldn't consider trading it for any other occupation. The food concession business is a well-kept secret, and we know we've got it made.

Ideally, your mistakes will be small, and you will move on to enjoy many years of profitable events.

Please, let me know where this book can be improved. I may be in the booth right next to yours.

Yours truly, proud of her first booth in 1984 (RV conversion).

APPENDIX 1

Planning Guide

For your new concession enterprise to be successful, you must plan and execute your actions carefully. This planning guide will help you foresee and plan your steps in an efficient manner. Some of the steps, such as acquiring your booth, designing equipment layout, and installing equipment, may take several months to complete. Allow yourself enough time to be ready for booking your events in the early spring.

Concept and Planning

- Attend events. (See chapter 2.)
- Talk to event coordinators and other vendors. (See chapter 2.)
- Define your goal. (See chapter 2.)
- Research menu ideas. List associated product and equipment and potential problems and benefits. (See chapter 4.)
- Research booth ideas. List potential types, designs, availability, and prices. (See chapter 5.)
- Research equipment. Visit used equipment dealers for ideas and prices. (See chapter 6.)
- Research sign ideas. (See chapter 6.)
- Contact state and county health departments. Request a mobile and temporary licensing manual. (See chapter 3.)
- Research vehicle options. (See chapter 7.)
- Determine your menu. List associated products, supplies, equipment, and small wares. Analyze preparation and serving scenario. (See chapter 4.)

- Determine product suppliers. (See chapter 4.)
- Plan storage needs for product and equipment during and between events. (See chapter 4.)
- Calculate start-up costs. (See chapter 8.)
- Arrange financing if needed. (See chapter 8.)
- Calculate a cost/profit analysis for each menu item. (See chapter 4.)
- Open a checking account specifically for your concession business. (See chapter 14.)
- Put together your business plan. (See chapter 2.)

Put It All Together

- Acquire your booth and design the equipment layout.
- Acquire major and minor equipment.
- Install equipment.
- Acquire vehicles.
- Acquire signs.
- Research potential events. Contact your department of tourism for an event guide. (See chapters 9 and 10.)
- Design your promotional flyer. (See chapter 10.)
- Contact event coordinators.
- Book events. (See chapter 10.)
- Acquire temporary restaurant permit applications. (See chapter 10.)
- Acquire insurance. (See chapter 3.)
- Acquire small wares. (See chapter 6.)
- Make labor arrangements. (See chapter 12.)
- Acquire miscellaneous supplies and lighting. (See chapter 11.)
- Set up a record-keeping system. (See chapter 14.)

It's Showtime

- Perform a dress rehearsal. (See chapter 10.)
- Purchase product and supplies. (See chapter 11.)
- Conduct a pre-trip inspection of all vehicles.

APPENDIX 2

FOOD VENDOR APPLICATION AND RELEASE   DONALD DAZE
JUNE 25-26 2005

NAME: _____ PHONE: _____
BUSINESS NAME: _____
ADDRESS: _____
CITY: _____STATE _____ZIP_____
EMAIL: _____

Describe items/food for sale: _____
_____
_____
_____

One 10'X10' space $50.00   Additional space $25.00
Sat Set-up 7am Open to Public 9am-5pm
Sun Set up 8am Open to Public 10am-4pm

ALL FEES ARE NON-REFUNDABLE   Number of Spaces Required: _____
APPLICATION DEADLINE: **MAY 30, 2005** (Please contact me if you are unable to meet the deadline & interested)

In consideration of my participation in Donald Daze, a non-profit community project, I hereby release Donald Daze, it's members, agents and officers, and each of them, from any and all liability for injury and or damage which may be incurred by me or as a result of, my participation in any activity or function sponsored, conducted or carried on by Donald Daze. Whether on public or private premises, and further hereby release any private host at and such function or activity forms any and all such liability. This release is binding on my heirs, administrators, representatives and assigns.

I HAVE READ THE FOREGOING REALEASE LIABILITY, UNDERSTAND IT'S CONTENTS, AND ACKNOWLDGE RECEIPT OF A COPY THERE OF. I (we) am/are at least 21 years of age. Please have everyone who will be working the booth sign and print their name. Thank You!!

Signature: _____
Print: _____
Date: _____ Amount Paid $ _____

Should you have any questions please feel free to contact me.

Every event has a different application. The form on this page and the next is an example of a typical two-page application and info sheet for a small community festival.

Donald Daze Guidelines
June 24-26 2005

TIME: Set up Sat 7 am till 8:45am
       Set up Sun 8 am till 9:45am
      OPEN TO THE PUBLIC Sat 9 am to 5 pm. (we ask that you do not leave early)
                    Sun 10 am to 4 pm

LOCATION: All along Main Street. Spaces will be marked and assigned on a first come basis

Vendors must be self-sufficient (with the exception of electricity), including tables, awnings, display rack, signs etc.

All merchandise for sale must be NEW (Antique items ok), No Flea market/garage sale items allowed.

Booths promoting, trading, stocking, or selling Guns, Knives, or any other weapons are NOT allowed.

We will make effort to prevent duplications of booths.

Food Vendors must be licensed by Health Department, Please cook with propane, generator, or barbeque when possible.

Water and electrical supplies are VERY limited

Booth participants are asked to bring their own garbage containers. A dumpster will be provided for trash bags.

Wheelchair access restrooms will be provided.

ALL VENDORS MUST PROVIDE THEIR OWN LIABILTY INSURANCE

Please enclose the correct registration fee with your booth application. Checks should be payable to: DONALD DAZE COMMITTEE

$25.00 for one 10' x 10' Space (Non Refundable)

$25.00 for each additional space, also non-refundable

PLEASE MAIL TO:

Donald, Or 97020

Call   'or more information

We are doing Booths on a first come first serve basis. We will block out all of the spaces and make sure that if you need multiple spaces in a row they are available.

If you know of anyone who would be interested in participating in DONALD DAZE please share this information and ask him or her to contact us. We are looking forward to seeing YOU

Firdale Food Company
Barb Fitzgerald, Owner/Operator
34680 SW Firdale Rd
Cornelius OR 97113
503/628-2090, fax 503/628-2090
firdale@earthlink.net

Greetings from Firdale Food Company. We are a small, service oriented company that specializes in quality food and friendly, professional service. For more than twenty years we have been proud to serve our delicious, freshly prepared menus at hundreds of the largest and best attended events in the Northwest.

In an effort to promote menu diversity at the events that we attend we offer two different menu options for you to choose from.

Menu Option #1

Curly Fries Giant fresh cut fries cooked to order. We special order a specific breed of potato to assure crispness.

Corn Dogs The best around.

All Natural Lemonade Our lemonade is made the old fashioned way-from scratch. Real fruit, fruit juice, sugar, and tea bags.

Lemon Ade
Strawberry Ade
Iced Tea
Arnold Palmer-
1/2 Iced tea, 1/2 Lemonade

Menu Option #2

Hand-Dipped Ice Cream Nut Bars
Select vanilla or chocolate ice cream. Dipped in chocolate and rolled in your choice of peanut bits, cheolate bits, or oreo cookie crumbs.

All Natural Thirst-Ade
Our beverages are made the old fashioned way—from scratch. Real fruit, fruit juice, sugar, and real tea bags.
Lemon Ade
Strawberry Ade
Raspberry Ade
Grape Ade
Iced Tea
Arnold Palmer—1/2 Iced tea, 1/2 Lemonade

We serve out of a 10x10 tent. In order to provide quality service and product to our customers we also use an 7x16 utility trailer that allows us easy access to stock, freezers, and washing facilities. Ideally, this trailer is set behind the tent. Our electrical requirements are 20 amps at 110 volts. We also need a direct hookup to fresh water.

Firdale Food Company is fully licensed and insured. Our staff is clean, friendly, and professional.

Thank you for considering us to serve at your event.

A document in the form of a flyer or brochure is designed to promote your business to event coordinators. It also gives them the important details of your business. This is just one example of what a promotional flyer might look like.

OREGON

TEMPORARY RESTAURANT LICENSE APPLICATION
AT LEAST ONE PERSON WITH A FOODHANDLER CARD MUST BE PRESENT AT ALL TIMES

Location of Event _____

Dates and Hours of Event _____

Business/Organization Name _____

Applicant's Name _____ Phone # _____

Mailing Address _____

Menu _____

When will food be prepared? _____

Where is food being purchased? _____

**THIS APPLICATION MUST BE COMPLETED IN FULL AND SUBMITTED WITH FEE TO
MARION COUNTY ENVIRONMENTAL HEALTH DEPARTMENT**

VIOLATIONS (OAR 333-150)

1. Person in charge not assigned or cannot demonstrate knowledge (2-101.11, 2-102.11)
2. Poor personal hygiene; eating, drinking, smoking (2-302.11,2-304.11,2-401.11,2-402.11)
3. Improper handwashing/use of hand sanitizers (2-301.11,2-301.16,5-203.11,5-205.11,6-301.11,6-301.12)
4. Ill employees (2-201.11-2-201.15,2-401.12)
5. No food handler certificate (OAR 333-175)
6. Food, ice, or water from unapproved sources (3-101.11,3-201.11-17,5-101.11)
7. Potentially hazardous food at improper temperatures (3-501.16)
8. Improper reheating or cooling of food (3-403.11,3-501.14,15)
9. Improper cooking of food (3-401.11-3-401.13)
10. Food not protected during transport, display, storage or preparation (3-302.11,3-303.11,12,3-305.11,12,3-305.14, 3-307.11,12)
11. Food-contact surfaces not clean and sanitized (3-304.11,4-601.11,4-602.11)
12. Nonfood-contact surfaces not clean (4-601.11,4-602.13)
13. Single service items not protected, dispensed or handled properly (4-903.11,4-904.11)
14. Thermometers not provided (4-204.112, 4-302.12)
15. Sanitizing cloths not provided, maintained (3-304.14)
16. Equipment and utensils improperly washed (4-301.12,13,4-603.15)
17. Improper disposal of solid and liquid wastes (5-403.11,5-503.11,5-501.13,5-502.11)

SPECIFIC PROBLEM(S) & REQUIRED CORRECTION(S)

_____
_____
_____
_____
_____
_____
_____

DO NOT WRITE IN THIS SPACE

FEE OF $ _____ RECEIPT # _____ DATE _____

OPERATOR _____ SANITARIAN _____ DATE _____

P:\TEMPORARY RESTAURANT LICENSE APPLICATION.doc

This is a typical temporary restaurant permit application. The top part is filled in duplicate and returned to the Health Department with payment. The health inspector will appear at the event with both copies, do an inspection using the lower portion of this same form, ask for your signature when the inspection is complete, and then leave you with a copy.

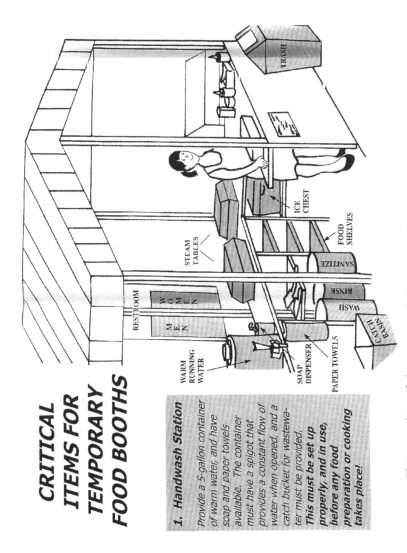

CRITICAL ITEMS FOR TEMPORARY FOOD BOOTHS

TRASH

ICE CHEST

FOOD SHELVES

STEAM TABLES

SANITIZE

RINSE

WASH

RESTROOM

WOMEN

MEN

WARM RUNNING WATER

SOAP DISPENSER

PAPER TOWELS

CATCH BASIN

1. Handwash Station

Provide a 5-gallon container of warm water, and have soap and paper towels available. The container must have a spigot that provides a constant flow of water when opened, and a catch bucket for wastewater must be provided. *This must be set up properly, and in use, before any food preparation or cooking takes place!*

This graphic of the essential elements of a temporary restaurant is a print-out from the Health Department guidebook.

Event Information Worksheet

Event: _____ _____Date:_____   Hours of Operation:_____

Location: *Park, street*_____ _____   Setup date/time:_____

Coordinator:_____ _____   Phone #:_____

Space Fee: *flat,%*_____ Deposit due date:_____   Insurance Cert. Due:_____

Health Dept. County:_____ __ Phone #:_____   Cost:_____

Utilities: *water, elec.*_____ _____Ice: Y____ N____   Camping/Parking: Y__ N__

Activities: *parade, crafts, carnival*_____

Menu:_____

Notes:_____

************************************ ** ***

Post Event Information

Expenses	Sales		Labor		
Space Fee_____	Date:	Amt:	Name:	date/time:	$
Health Permit_____	_____	_____	_____	_____	_____
Fuel_____	_____	_____	_____	_____	_____
Supplies_____	_____	_____	_____	_____	_____
Labor_____	_____	_____	_____	_____	_____
Propane_____	_____	_____	_____	_____	_____
Total_____	Total_____		_____	_____	_____

Inventory Used: _____

Notes: *# of booths, weather, attendance,space location etc.* _____

Event information is first gleaned from the coordinator over the phone or from the event application packet. Record space fees and deposits. Once the event is complete, expenses, sales and labor figures will be available for record. Each vendor may have considerations particular to their situation and should customize the form accordingly.

Event Schedule 2004

Event	Dates	worker 1	worker 2
Fun Days	May 14-16	Fri 4pm-10pm	
		Sat. 10am-8pm	
		Sun 10-close	
Good Times	June 18-20	Fri 4pm-10pm	
		Sat. all	
		Sun. optional	
Fireworks Day	July-04	Sun. 9am-close	Sun 9am- 9pm
Recovery Days	July 9-11	Fri 4pm-10pm	
		Sat. 10am-10pm	Sat 10am-6pm
		Sun. 11am-close	
Fat City Days	July 15-18	Thurs. 12-10	
		Fri.. 10-10	Fri. 6pm-10pm
		Sat. 10-10	Sat. 10am-10pm
		Sun 10-close	
Big Bucks Days	July 22-25	Thurs. 5pm-10pm	
		Fri. 10am-10pm	
		Sat. 10am-10pm	Sat 10am-10pm
		Sun. 10 am-close	
Town Bash	July 31-Aug 1	Sat. 9am-7pm	
		Sun. 9am-close	
Concert	Aug. 7-8	Sat. 9am-7pm	
		Sun. 9am-close	
Rodeo	Aug 12-15	Thurs. 12-10pm	
		Fri. 10am-10pm	Fri. 6pm-10pm
		Sat. 10am-10pm	Sat. 10am-10pm
		Sun. 10 am-close	
Auction	Sept. 3-5	Fri. 10am-6pm	
		Sat. 10am-6pm	
		Sun. 10am-close	
Labor Days	Sept 11-12	Sat. 10am-10pm	
		Sun. optional	

A simple event schedule ensures that everyone knows exactly where and when they are scheduled to work.

Event Income Statement
Year _____

	Event #1	Event #2	Event #3	Event #4	Event #5	Total
Event Name						
Sales						
Cost of Sales						
Gross Profit from Sales						

Event Expenses

Space Fee						
Health Permit						
Fuel						
Propane						
Contract Labor						
Camping/Motel						
Other						

Total Expenses

Profit/Loss						
Year to Date						

An event statement tracks each event's sales and expenses. The numbers across the top are for each of four events.

Monthly Expense Log

Month_____ Year_____

Date	Payee/ check #	Stock	Permits	Space Fees	Fuel & Propane	Labor	Repairs & Maint.	Office	Utilities	Ins.	Other
Totals											

An expense ledger logs business expenses through the month. The figures are taken from your receipt jar, checkbook ledger, and credit card statement.

Profit and Loss Statement

Year _____

	May	June	July	Aug	Sept	Total
Sales						
Cost of Sales						
Gross Profit from Sales						
Event Expenses						
Space Fees						
Health Permits						
Fuel						
Propane						
Utilities						
Contract Labor						
Motel/Camping						
Other						
Total Event Expenses						
Operating Expenses						
Repairs & Maintenance						
Insurance						
Office Supplies						
Utilities						
Finance Charges						
Total Operating Expenses						
Total Expenses						
Profit/Loss						

A profit and loss ledger extends the monthly expense log over the season.

Example Inventory Audit

Event_____ Date _____ to _____

Date_____	16oz Cups $2.00	24oz Cups $3.00	Trays $3.00	Tissues $2.00
Starting	150			
(minus) Ending	100			
(equals) Out	50			
Value $	100			
Total Receipts $	94			
Over/Short $	6			

Date_____	16oz Cups $2.00	24oz Cups $3.00	Trays $3.00	Tissues $2.00
Starting				
(minus) Ending				
(equals) Out				
Value $				
Total Receipts $				
Over/Short $				

Date_____	16oz Cups $2.00	24oz Cups $3.00	Trays $3.00	Tissues $2.00
Starting				
(minus) Ending				
(equals) Out				
Value $				
Total Receipts $				
Over/Short $				

Date_____	16oz Cups $2.00	24oz Cups $3.00	Trays $3.00	Tissues $2.00
Starting				
(minus) Ending				
(equals) Out				
Value $				
Total Receipts $				
Over/Short $				

Performing an inventory audit prior to opening and after closing will verify that the product used up during the day balances with the day's sales receipts. In this case, the four items listed represent two sizes of pop, a chili dog, and a hot dog with their respective sales price. The first column is filled in as an example.

Example Yearly Event Comparison

Event Name										
1985		119	821					331		
1986		299	355					953		
1987		556	767	960				1130		
1988		355						2112		
1989		1146	1341	1889				3364		
1990		1463	1620					3475		1007
1991		1887	1585	2006				2625		
1992		1571	1947	1542	2831			2153		
1993		1633	2385	2127	3500			4400		
1994	1039		1086	610	944			1558		
1995		293	1019	754				1090	1901	
1996		881	724	1905				3783	1842	
1997	1053	1200	4393	2437				4762	2505	
1998		1835	4341	3198		2910		6989	4673	3734
1999	2520	2211	2774	3088		2173		5883	4541	1889
2000	2027	2559	2838	2074		3172	2417	5294	3322	1418
2001	2684	2892	3736	1942		2900	1533	5262		
2002	2431	3700	3683		4478		2268	4715	2863	2035
2003	2500	3484	3795		5071		2885	5014	2935	2163
2004	1886	3561	4086	1951	4314	3300	2505	5734	3383	2359

A yearly event comparison tracks the performance of each season's events over several years.

APPENDIX 3: REFERENCES

Associations

The following associations are a rich source of information about the industry. Many of these websites have event listings, insurance agency listings, news updates on regulation legislature, supply sources, lists, and links to other associations, and much more.

California Department of Food and Agriculture, www.cdfa.ca.gov/fe/

California Fair Services Authority, www.cfsa.org

Canada Association of Fairs and Expositions, www.canadian-fairs.ca

IAFA, International Association of Fairs and Expositions, www.fairsandexpos.com

NICA, National Independent Concessionaires Association, Inc. www.nicainc.org

Texas Association of Fairs and Events, www.texasfairs.com

Washington State Fair Association, www.wastatefairs.com

Western Fairs Association, www.fairsnet.org

Concession Trailer and Pushcart Manufacturers

Century Industries, www.centuryindustries.com

Concession Connection, www.concessionconnection.com

Concession Trailers, www.concession-trailers.com, classified listings of concession trailers and pushcarts.

Creative Mobile Systems, www.cmssystem.com

Custom Products, www.customsalesandservice.com

Ohio Trailer Supply, www.ohiotrailer.com

Pace American Trailers, www.hgrstrailer.com

Sno-Balls Trailer Manufacturing, www.snow-balls.com

Supreme Products, www.supremeproducts.com

Waymatic, www.waymatic.com

Wells Cargo, www.wellscargo.com, the most popular concession trailer manufacturer.

Concession Tent Manufacturers

Anchor Industries Inc. www.anchorinc.com

B&B Manufacturing, www.bnbpartytents.com

Craft Canopy, www.craftcanopy.com

Event Tec, www.toptecinc.com

EZ-Up Canopies, www.ezupdirect.com

Main Awning and Tent, www.tentsource.com

PTM Canopy, 888/343-6789, www.ptmcanopy.com

Event Listings Guides

Art and Craft Shows, www.artandcraftshows.net searchable database of art festivals and craft shows.

Arts and crafts show business, www.artscraftsshowbusiness.com, Southeastern States, 904/757-3913.

Craft Master News, www.craftmasternews.com, Western States.

Craft Shows USA, www.craftshowsusa.com Home and garden shows, wine festivals, quilt shows.

The Department of Tourism in your state for an event guide/ annual calendar of events.

Festival Finder, www.festivalfinder.com, more than 2,500 music festivals in North America.

Festival Net, www.festivalnet.com Nationwide craft show, art fair, music festival and event guide.

Mike and Pat's, www.newenglandcraftshows.com, Mike and Pat's craft fairs.

National events directory, www.nationaleventsdirectory.com Information of special interest to concessionaires.

Shows for Vendors, www.showsforvendors.com, Western States.

South Fest, www.SouthFest.com, festival listings for the south, including GA, FL, NC, SC, TN, VA, and more.

Smart Frogs, www.smartfrogs.com, N.E States, 888/918-1313.

Sugar Loaf, www.sugarloafcrafts.com, juried fine art and craft festivals since 1976.

Where It's at Magazine, www.whereitsatmagazine.com, Southern States, 512/926-7954.

Business Information

Canadian Government website for food service licensing,http://www.inspection.gc.ca/english/related/restaure.shtml

Contact the Secretary of State's Office or website in your state for a business guide.

IRS, 800/829-3676, www.irs.gov

U.S. Small Business Administration, www.sbaonline.sba.gov

www.homefoodsafety.com, a good educational site on safe food handling procedures.

Insurance Agencies

The following is a brief list of insurance agencies listed on Fairsnet.org. or found through other channels:

Advanced Insurance/Emory Frink, Special Programs for Food Concessionaires. Former concessionaires who understands your business. 714/997-8100, 800/655-4033

Allied Specialty Insurance, Inc., Provides comprehensive, affordable, custom-designed insurance to the amusement industry. Fairs and expositions, amusement parks, water facilities, and independent concession operators. 800/237-3355, 813/367-6900

Haas and Wilkerson Insurance, Inc. The largest independently-owned producer of entertainment insurance in the U.S. Providing for independent concessionaires and almost every kind of special event.

Insurance Exchange/Monty Coleman, 800/929-0172, 503/538-2148

Food Service Product Suppliers

Boxer Northwest, 800/547-5700, www.boxernw.com

Costco, www.costco.com

Food Service of America, www.foodserviceofamerica.com

Hubert, 800/543-7374, www.hubert.com

Johnson's Restaurant Supply, 800/452-7684

Katom Restaurant Supply, www.katom.com

Rose's Equipment and Supply, Inc., 503/233-7450

Superior Products/U.S. Foodservice, 800/328-9800, www.superprod.com

Sysco, www.sysco.com, 1-800/776-8904

United Grocers, 503/833-1000

Unified Western Grocers, www.uwgrocers.com

Food Service Equipment Manufacturers and Suppliers

Amana, www.amana.com

Cambro, www.cambro.com

Frymaster, www.frymaster.com

Hamilton Beach, www.hamiltonbeach.com

Jean's Restaurant Supply, www.jeansrestaurantsupply.com

Jet Spray, www.cornelius.com

Manitowoc, www.manitowoc.com

Pitco, www.pitco.com

Restaurant Equipment and Supply, www.restaurantequipment.com

Scotsman Artic Air, www.articair.com

Server Products, www.server-products.com

Southern Concession Supply, www.scpopcorn.com

Vita Mix, www.vitamix.com

Vollrath, www.vollrathco.com

Vittitow Refrigeration, www.vittitow.com

ABOUT THE AUTHOR

Barb Fitzgerald has over twenty years of experience in the food concession business. She has successfully designed and operated a variety of concession operations and has served a large assortment of menus at hundreds of events in the Northwest. In addition to running her concession business, she also designed and operated a successful espresso café for Portland Oregon's Tri-Met transit system.

In 1994, Barb was honored to become involved in the administrative and regulatory process by co-chairing a position on the Oregon Food Services Advisory Board as representative for the food concession industry. It was that experience that inspired her to found NWVN, Northwest Vendor's Network, an association of vendors and event coordinators for the purpose of improving communication and cooperation among associates in the concession industry.

The advice of this busy professional has been sought by many event organizers, and she has served as consultant to many concession entrepreneurs. Her dedicated entrepreneurship, accumulated experience in concession development, management and marketing, and passion for the concession business qualify her as a concession operations authority.

Barb lives on a Registered Historic Farmstead in Oregon, where she pursues a simple organic lifestyle. Her hobbies include gardening and kayaking.

INDEX

Give the Gift of

Food Booth

The Entrepreneur's Complete Guide to
the Food Concession Business

to Your Friends and Colleagues

CHECK YOUR LEADING BOOKSTORE OR ORDER HERE

❏ **YES**, I want _____ copies of *Food Booth* at $34.95 each, plus $5.00 shipping per book. Canadian orders must be accompanied by a postal money order in US funds. Allow 15 days for delivery.

My check or money order for $_____ is enclosed.

Please charge my: ❏ Visa ❏ MasterCard
❏ Discover ❏ American Express

Name _____

Organization _____

Address _____

City/State/Zip _____

Phone_____ Email _____

Card # _____

Exp. Date_____ Signature _____

Please make your check payable and return to:
Carnival Press
P.O. Box 1068 • Cornelius, OR 97113

Call your credit card order toll-free to: 1-800-376-5074

Fax: (503) 628-2090 **Order Online at: www.foodbooth.net**